ENCOUNTERS WITH CHINESE WRITERS

Lucy from Jane White
Nov 26, 2009

ALSO BY ANNIE DILLARD

ENCOUNTERS WITH CHINESE WRITERS

ANNIE DILLARD

WESLEYAN UNIVERSITY PRESS

WESLEYAN UNIVERSITY PRESS

Published by University Press of New England,
Hanover, NH 03755

Copyright © 1984 by Annie Dillard

Printed in the United States of America   5   4   3

∞

Some of these narratives have appeared in *Harvard Magazine,*
Radcliffe Quarterly, and *Harper's Magazine.*

LIBRARY OF CONGRESS CATALOGING IN PUBLICATION DATA

Dillard, Annie.
Encounters with Chinese writers.

1. Authors, Chinese—20th century—Anecdotes, facetiae,
satire, etc. I. Title.
PL2277.D54   1984   895.1'09'005   84-7322
ISBN 0-8195-5130-9 (alk. paper)
ISBN 0-8195-6156-8 (pbk.: alk. paper)

For Phyllis

AUTHOR'S NOTE

Like most writers who deal with contemporary China, I've disguised some people. Wu Fusan is not the man's real name, nor is Song Hua, Mr. Fu, or Sam Samson. All the other major characters appear under their actual names.

Throughout, I've used standard Pinyin spelling—"Beijing, Hangzhou"—except where long usage dictates older forms—"Peking Hotel."

For support, information, and valuable opinion, I am grateful to the National Endowment for the Arts, to the National Committee on United States–China Relations, to Irving Lo (Department of East Asian Languages and Cultures, Indiana University), Jeannette Hopkins (Wesleyan University Press), Perry Link (Department of East Asian Languages and Cultures, UCLA), Robert Rees, Donald Ellegood, my husband Gary Clevidence, André Schiffrin (Pantheon Books), and Phyllis Rose.

CONTENTS

INTRODUCTION

These are anecdotes—sketches—of encounters in China and in the United States with various Chinese people, many of them established writers.

The encounters in China took place in May and June 1982. I was travelling as a member of a six-person delegation of U.S. scholars, writers, and publishers. The other delegates were Irving Lo, Indiana University; James Liu, Stanford University; Leopold Tyrmand, the Rockford Institute; André Schiffrin, Pantheon Books; and Donald Ellegood, University of Washington Press. We spent ten days in Beijing meeting with writers; then we travelled to Xian, Hangzhou, Nanjing, and Shanghai. The first part of this book tells some stories from that trip.

There is a toasting scene at a banquet; a scene with a bitter diplomat at a dance hall; a formal meeting with Chinese writers; a conversation with an American businessman in a hotel lobby; an evening with long-suffering intellectuals in their house; the almost obligatory encounter with a worker on the street in Shanghai; a scene of unwarranted hilarity in the Beijing Library; and a scene in the Beijing foreigners' compound with an excited European journalist and his family. There is also some information about Chinese literary life, publishing, economics, and family life.

These are mostly anecdotes—moments—from which few generalizations may be drawn except perhaps about Chinese—and human—complexity. Their subject is not China *per se*; their subject is the paradoxical nature of all of our days, the curious way we bump up against the unexpected everywhere, the endless dramas of good will in bad times, the sheer comedy of human differences and cultural differences, and the courage and even whimsy with which we—all of us—cope.

I read some of these anecdotes as the Phi Beta Kappa Oration at Harvard/Radcliffe commencement exercises in 1983. *Harvard Magazine* and *Radcliffe Quarterly* published what I read, and many people wrote to congratulate me for "telling the truth about China." Their generosity flattered me, but I cannot pretend to understand what they meant. Can a sheaf of snapshots show "the truth"? The truth about China I leave to the experts. I intend only to tell some small stories, and to depict precise moments precisely, in the hope that a collection of such moments might give an impression of many sharp points going in different directions—might give a vivid sense of complexity. The narratives and analyses in this section are not value-free, of course, but they yield, I hope, contradictory impressions.

I am writing here for the general reader. I pray the Sinologist will forgive the evident naïveté of some of these stories, with their retelling of paradoxes and horrors long familiar to everyone in the field.

The second part of *Encounters with Chinese Writers* presents a small group of Chinese writers travelling in the United States.

In September 1982, four months after my visit to China, I met a delegation of Chinese writers in Los Angeles. Norman Cousins had organized a four-day U.S.-Chinese writers conference, and I was one of the U.S. delegates. The other U.S. delegates were Allen Ginsberg, Francine du Plessix

Gray, John Hersey, Jerome Lawrence, Robert E. Lee, Arthur Miller, Harrison Salisbury, Gary Snyder, and Kurt Vonnegut.

The Chinese writers were, for the most part, real writers and not just functionaries. They were Feng Mu, Wu Qiang, Li Ying, Li Zhun, Jiang Zilong, Zhang Jie, and interpreter Yuan Henian. (I list them by rank, Chinese-style; similarly, in China we Americans were always listed, introduced, and seated by "rank.") The conference included many other participants and special guests. I'd met two of the Chinese writers before. Now here they were again, sprung exhilarated from China, and here were the same events: formal meetings about writers' goals and cultural differences, and informal moments of comedy or collusion.

By day we all worked the hi-tech big stage together. We spoke to a darkened auditorium from behind a long, U-shaped conference table; before us were stationary microphones, and at our ears were headsets for simultaneous translations. By night we partied. We were entertained at various elaborate houses up and down the Southern California coast: at Norman Lear's, at Norman Cousins', at Jerome Lawrence's. I myself had rarely seen such conspicuous luxury anywhere; the Chinese, fresh from Beijing, took it in stride. There were only seven of them, a varied lot, and all warm and spirited; we became friends.

When the conference broke up, Allen Ginsberg and I stayed an extra day to accompany the Chinese writers to Disneyland. Then we all scattered. Over the next three weeks the Chinese writers worked their way, lecturing and sightseeing, to the East Coast. From New York they drove to Middletown, Connecticut, and had dinner with me at home. The next day I set off with them for Massachusetts.

We visited Walden Pond. They hadn't heard of Thoreau, but liked what they learned. Standing at the site of Thoreau's cabin, the very distinguished delegation leader, Feng Mu, said, "I think if I came here I would stay not just one year, but ten years." He looked out at the pond, breathing expansively. He was wearing an oversized raincoat and a brimmed hat with half a dozen bright red maple and verbena leaves stuck in the hatband. He added, with a pleased look, "But I would leave every winter."

It was ordinary sightseeing, such as we'd done in Disneyland. I was charmed to note the Chinese writers' sprinting off in every direction—to pick up pretty leaves, or buy souvenirs, or make phone calls, joke with each other, cross busy streets at whim, daydream—just as we Americans had done in China, secretly preening ourselves on this putative national characteristic. I was enlightened to hear the same exasperation in the American guides' voices: Stay with the group, please; stay with the group. The next day we went on to Harvard.

By then I'd done some reading, and was less easily surprised by things Chinese, and more interested in exploring the warmth and subtlety of these new friends than in trying to get to the bottom of "the truth about China." We were relaxed, even exuberant: at one Boston restaurant we amused ourselves by balancing spoons on our noses. At dawn on the campus of Wesleyan University we tomfooled around calling out marching cadences and marching. In Connecticut, as in Disneyland, we danced.

What we have in the second part is some information and analysis and, again, a series of snapshots: the lovely young

Zhang Jie suiting abrupt mood changes to a variety of actions; Allen Ginsberg having a bewildering conversation in Disneyland with a cosmopolitan Chinese journalist; the handsome young Jiang Zilong, singing in a Connecticut dining room with his eyes closed.

These are only glimpses, not portraits; their subject is not China, and not even entirely Chinese writers, but a few vivid, equivocal moments in the days of some of earth's people in the twentieth century. What interests me here, and elsewhere, is the possibility for a purified nonfiction narration—a kind of Chekhovian storytelling which might illuminate the actual world with a delicate light—coupled with humor in the American tradition and no comment.

PART ONE

A MAN OF THE WORLD

We are being feted at a banquet in Beijing, in one of a restaurant's many private banquet rooms. The room is drab and charmless; the food is wonderful.

Our hosts, members of the Beijing Writers Association, are mostly men and women in their fifties, sixties, seventies, and eighties. They are people who have witnessed, participated in, and in some cases sacrificed for, the liberation of China. In their early lives they saw civil war, and world war, and foreign occupation, and more civil war—all turning around in January 1949, when Mao's Communists, many of them veterans of the 1935 Long March, walked into Beijing. They deposed the local warlords and made it their capital. By the fall of that year they had taken the big port cities on the east coast. It was all over, essentially, but the shouting, which has continued on and off ever since. The Cultural Revolution, which lasted ten years until 1976, was only the most recent and ruinous of a series of internal purgative campaigns. Most of the Chinese people in this room, as intellectuals, were to various degrees among the Cultural Revolution's victims. Some of them, however, were bureaucrats who were canny enough to stay out of trouble.

My attention now is on one of our many hosts, seated beside me. Wu Fusan, I will call him, is a politically powerful man in his late sixties or seventies. I have watched him in action for days; he is the sharpest of sharpies, the smoothest of smoothies. The others at the table interest me more, I think, but here he is—beside me, speaking English.

Wu Fusan is a tall, soft-voiced old man with a ready,

mirthless laugh. His arms are long; his fingers are light and knobbed, like bamboo. He wears a tailored gray jacket. He jokes a lot, modestly, about his powerful position. When he laughs, his face splits open at the jaw, revealing a lot of gum and teeth. His white hair is just long enough in front to hold the suggestion of a part; the hair shoots out diagonally in two directions from this part, giving him a windblown look, as if he were perpetually standing in the bow of a ship.

He is infinitely relaxed. He lounges in his chair; he tilts back his long head and brings out his words slowly, crooningly, from deep in his throat. He makes no effort to be heard; if you want to hear him, you must lean into him and lower your head, as if you were bowing. We chat.

His eyes do not seem to be involved in his words at all. Instead, from their tilted-back position, his eyes are studying you with a bored, distant, amused look—the way we would watch Saturday-morning cartoons on television for a minute or two, if we had to. He laughs his mirthless laugh at whatever you say, and at whatever he says, as if some greatly successful joke has been made, or some wonderful coincidence has been discovered, which makes the two of you accomplices. Usually this is the laugh of a nervous woman in society—but the woman uses her eyes, and Wu Fusan does not. He nods vigorously and tightens his legs; he is absolutely breathless with laughter; the lower half of his face is broken with laughter; he murmurs "Yes, Yes," in an educated British accent—and his eyes continue their bored appraisal. I have written him off as a hack, a politico, a man of the world without depth or interest. I am, as usual, wrong.

I learn later that Wu Fusan's class background is excellent: his father was a poor peasant. I learn still later—in a manner I will shortly relate—that his personal background is so impeccable that in the Cultural Revolution he lost only his books. Red Guards confiscated them because he spoke English and was known to have relatives overseas.

It is rude to drink alone in China. When someone at your table wants to drink his *mao-tai*, he raises his glass to you, and you are obliged to drink with him. Our host, Wu Fusan, has offered several formal toasts to us foreign guests seated at this table. Now, as the conversation splinters, and the beautiful, fragrant dishes pass before us one by one, he raises his tiny crystal glass to me, and we drink.

As we drink, Wu holds my eyes. As we lower our glasses and tilt them briefly towards each other, Wu holds my eyes. There is something extraordinary in his look. This occurs a dozen times over the course of the banquet; I have ample opportunity to see just how extraordinary this look is.

The man is taking my measure. He is measuring what I can only call my "spirit"—my "depths," such as they are. No one has ever looked at me this way. There is nothing personal or flirtatious about it. He is going into my soul with calipers. He is entering my eyes as if they were a mineshaft; he is testing my spirit with a plumb line.

His gaze is calm and interested. He is not looking at my face, nor my eyes, in any usual way; he is not particularly even looking at me. He is examining something inside me; he gauges my "strength" as if he were counting the coils of a loaded spring. All this takes less than a minute. We put our glasses down. The first time it happens, I think, What on earth was *that* all about? But there is no time to think about it; we resume small talk around the table. With us are other "literary workers"—Chinese and American publishers, scholars, and writers.

Every time we drink together, Wu Fusan and I, it happens again, and I learn more. I hate to think what *he* is learning—but I won't lower my eyes. I let him look; I hide nothing. What's to hide? I don't even know *how* to hide. You need to know, I think, that the ideas to which I have committed my life have required no more effort of me than occasional trips to the library. My life has set me at little risk, put me under no hardship. In this, I and many Americans my age differ from most of the world's people. I am a light-hearted woman born at the end of World War II into American peace and plenty. He can see all this easily, I believe. I wonder why he bothers. I think it is a habit with him. The conversation is desultory.

My strongest impression is this: that Wu Fusan has been down this particular well—the well of the human spirit—many times, and he can go a hell of a lot farther. The deeper he goes, the more interested he gets, but, I stress, his is an analytical interest, and, I stress, he hits bottom. My depths are well within reach of his plumb line. He pays out his line slowly, drink by drink, double-checking, and gets his answer. I wish I were deeper, but there you are.

His look is neither sexual nor combative, although there was considerable sizing up involved. He was sizing up my spirit, my heart and strength, my capacity for commitment. This is what counts to a Maoist—in a friend and in an enemy—why shouldn't he be in the habit of looking for it?

Still, it was an odd, unverifiable impression for me to have, and I doubted it. It was too vague, internal, and groundless to count as anything but imagination.

Later I met a woman in China whose thinking I trusted. She was an Italian who had lived in China for years and had close Chinese friends. I tried to describe to her Wu Fusan's deep, measuring look.

"That's right," she said. "That's what they do. You weren't imagining it. This is their great area of expertise. Have you read much Chinese literature? Most of it, for thousands of years, is about this one thing: the human spirit in all its depth and complexity. Whole stories hinge on some small human variation, some quirk of the interior life. There is nothing they do not already understand. It makes them peaceful, at ease with all people. When I am alone with a Chinese man, I am as peaceful as if I were alone with only myself. Everything is known. Western men," she added unexpectedly, and not unsympathetically, "cannot see any of this."

Now the waitress brings the final soup to our banquet table. We are chatting politely. I am not thinking of our extraordinary toasting; I will sort all that out later. Not much is being said. Wu Fusan continues his paroxysms of social laughter, clapping his bony hands on his bony knees. Is this your first visit to China? We hope you will soon return.

I ask Wu where he's from. This is a standard polite question in China. He is not from Beijing, he says; he is from Sichuan Province—which is over 1,000 miles away. Paying very little attention, I continue.

"How long have you lived in Beijing?"

Unexpectedly he gives me a little amused glance and shrugs.

"Since we took it."

THE MEETING

We are meeting with members of a big-city branch of the Chinese Writers Association, with publishers and editors, scholars, writers, and translators. There are six of us—American scholars, publishers, and writers. There are sixteen of them, our Chinese hosts—men in their fifties, sixties, or seventies. We all shake hands.

From the dark, decrepit hallway we have been shown into this light, odd meeting room. Every office building in China seems to have one like it. Against each wall are enormous overstuffed chairs and couches, square, matching, with lace antimacassars and doilies. There is new, red velvet upholstery. The windows are curtainless. Sit down!

Here we all are—we foreigners, eager to please, to extend the hand of friendship, to enjoy a meeting of minds, to sell books. And here they all are—these handsome and alert men, sitting smiling and at various degrees of ease in their red velvet chairs.

They are China's literary establishment, an establishment which includes, as does ours, some people who have long since abandoned art for politics and for the preservation and enjoyment of their reputations, people whose good manners, personal connections, and canniness have buoyed them to the top. Unlike ours, however, China's literary establishment carries a top-heavy freight of publishers, political critics, and bureaucrats, many of whom wield real power. There are also active writers, writers whose passions are literary and whose ambitions are for the quality of their work.

The head man, an old pro, is relaxed. He smokes; he jokes; he knows he can get through this just fine. After all, he plays host to over sixty such foreign delegations a year. He is paid to do this; he is what the Chinese call a *waiban*, wittily translated as a "barbarian handler." The others, lower-ranked and younger, seem less certain. They sit oddly on the edge of their chairs, ankles crossed. Some literary matters are touchy issues in China. And one must, at a formal meeting, be polite to foreigners without seeming to like them.

"Welcome to our group," the head man says. It begins. The interpreters lean forward, concentrating. While we remain seated, there are introductions all around, in order of rank, with titles—the deputy director, the vice editor, the deputy editor-in-chief. The men are all wearing Sun Yatsen jackets, blue or gray, of very fine cotton, tailored and lined. Those of higher rank will eventually loosen their collars; the day is hot.

We learn, over the morning, more things about these people: this one taught at Brown, that one is translating *The Leatherstocking Tales*, and most of them have been in prison.

Not in the room, of course, are any of the young writers and editors of those unofficial literary magazines which flourished for a year or so until 1980, when police closed them. (One such magazine was halted after its ninth issue, which contained such manifestoes as "the starting point of poetry should be the poet's self," and "I'm opposed to the stranglehold on people's souls by a stereotyped style.")

We have all acknowledged introductions by nodding. The head man lights another cigarette. "Let's have an informal meeting this morning. Here are, for example, Mr. Wu and Mr. Zhang, very active today in literature, and both very humorous people." There is a pause. The Chinese stiffen.

Today the usual tea-serving maids do not seem to be available, so the woman writer pours the tea. There is always one woman. She may have the second-highest rank in the room, or she may have written the novel most admired all over China. It takes her fifteen minutes to pour the tea, and she will do this three or four times in the course of the morning. After she serves, she takes an inconspicuous seat, sometimes on the one little hard chair stuck behind the real chairs.

If she is forced to speak, she smiles continuously, ducking her head, perhaps covering her mouth out of bashfulness, and laughing disarmingly between phrases, as if she simply cannot help the silliness of her remarks. Later at an evening banquet she will calmly drink everyone under the table, make pointed and even sarcastic cracks, and hold my bare arm in the sweetest, most natural way.

Now there is a meeting at hand. It will last all morning. Tea has been served.

"It is cool today in comparison to tomorrow," our host offers through a young interpreter. We can only agree.

After a brief introduction to the production unit at hand, and all its pomps and works, we are let loose to ask questions. Our host has already discovered from other meetings with us that we are harmless; we are too ignorant to cause damage. For them it is, I think, like talking to young children about what you did in the war. Whatever you did, the memory of which might be quite painful to you, will fortunately never be touched on by the children's little questions, always so innocently wide of the mark. Their own futures, for some, may depend on their positions on national literary issues—for example, may a story's hero, whose revolutionary ideals are correct, have flaws?—but we don't have the sense to ask such questions, and we have the courtesy not to press points. We want to know what it is about Herman Wouk that obsesses them so, and how manuscripts are chosen for publication, and in what sort of theoretical framework writers are composing. (If we had no chance to talk to real writers about real issues, or about craft, that is simply the nature of formal groups. The Chinese writers I travelled with later in the United States had no such chance either, and it frustrated them.) The conversation had a pleasingly surreal quality, largely because we constantly questioned people outside their areas of expertise— as if a Chinese writer were to ask an American publishing house sales manager about prosody, or, more aptly, as if a Chinese writer were to quiz an aspiring American novelist about Chinese literature.

"We have translated into Chinese many works of literary criticism from Europe and the United States. For example, Aristotle's *Poetics*."

"Speaking personally, I am very fond of contemporary American fiction. For example, *Rebecca*."

Someone uses the phrase "human nature," and there is a bewildering explosion of laughter. It is nervous laughter. For it turns out that "human nature" is the key phrase in what is at the moment the key issue, the heart of the political controversy. Mao said that there is no such thing as "human nature;" there is only class nature. To talk about human nature is, then, to undermine the theoretical basis of socialism.

Actually there is a nice continuity between classical Chinese literature and Communist Chinese literature. It is an old Confucian idea that literature should serve the state. Confucius himself is said to have edited (or censored) Chinese literature: he read more than 3,000 poems for an anthology—the *Book of Songs*, which contains only 305 poems—rejecting those which were not "serviceable" to the social order.

At any rate, we learn that literary life in China is very much in flux. Foreign writing is pouring in, at apparent random: Theodore Dreiser, Joyce Carol Oates, Agatha Christie, Mark Twain, Bernard Malamud, Sydney Sheldon, Irving Wallace, Benjamin Franklin. Yet Chinese writers are still mostly confined to writing fiction about idealized workers, peasants, and soldiers.

We ask around the room: What are your goals as a writer? We get a series of thoughtful answers, charmingly translated:

"The goals of my writing are like the goals of others: to help the understanding of the people, or perhaps to travel."

"To hold a mirror up to life."

"To raise the level of the people about science and technology."

"To write for the people. I ask myself, 'What is the requirement of the people?' But most of all, the real world."

"I am interested in the relationship between art and idea. My works have three main ideas:

one, that history is created by laboring people;

two, that China can exist as a nation;

and three, where to go next? In my short stories I try to answer the question of young people, where to go next."

In fact, Chinese writers can do both more and less than they're telling.

One man, whose wife is a high official, has been experimenting with stream-of-consciousness technique. One woman, who is a Party member, is able to deal with some real social problems in her work, such as the Chinese feminist issue: if the state requires a woman to work, how can she give enough time to her family? On the other hand, when a poet, in a little poem, likened the Yellow River to a shroud, it made a sensation: how patriotic is that? Even foreign writers have the sense to praise their rivers: the Mississippi, the Danube, the Don. What goals could possibly be served by running down the Yellow River with such a negative simile?

Only later will we begin to understand how poignant are the *unstated* goals of many writers: to have their work known outside China, published just as they wrote it, and judged on its literary merits alone.

The Chinese Writers Associations do not pretend to be communities of artists, or craft guilds, or unions. There is no hypocrisy here. The state established them to organize, subsidize, and to some extent control the people who will serve China's goals by writing.

Every short story in China, every novel, play, or movie, and every poem, has a clear purpose, which is to serve the goal of modernization. This is also the function of every shoe in China, every tree, every television set, cartwheel, flywheel, airplane, ditch. By extension, this is also the function of every novelist, poet, cobbler, wheelwright, baby, pilot, ditchdigger.

Chinese writers live with the idea of sacrifice, and the fact of sacrifice, and we do not; so talking is difficult. Chinese writers live with the idea of their country's future, and with the fact of many recent lives sacrificed for that future, and we do not. For what have we sacrificed? We well-fed writers are free to take potshots at our institutions from our couches.

It is true to say that the state imposes its goals on writers, but it is more true, I think, to note, as Sinologist Vera Schwarcz does, that in the recent past intellectuals have deliberately and in full consciousness accepted those goals, for the love of China, and accepted the Party's right to impose goals, and accepted even the sacrifice of their own independent thought, for the love of China. The task is to make China work as a harmonious, prosperous, and equitable modern nation—by dint of will, expertise, cooperation, sacrifice, passion, and the accumulation of capital.

"I believe," says one man, "that after several decades we will be able to lead a good life on our soil." He is speaking of his goals as a writer, and he is addressing the point directly.

He is a handsome man, and an elegant one in his trim gray jacket. He sits erect and relaxed, often with a disdainful expression; when he laughs, his face crumples surprisingly into a series of long dimples. He writes scathing criticism of the government. He is not laughing now, nor is he disdainful. The very contraction and repose of his limbs suggest great passion under great control. He repeats, "I believe that after several decades we will be able to lead a good life on our soil."

Ah, that soil! He has put his finger on it. For the main fact and difficulty of China is its millions of square miles of terrible soil, soil that all the will and cooperation in the world cannot alter. He has put his finger on it, and so have many others—for the soil in this populous region is so clay-like, and the technology for working it so labor-intensive, that it—the soil—actually has fingerprints on it.

Driving to this meeting we saw fields on the outskirts of the city, and patches of agriculture. There was a field of eggplant. Separating the rows of eggplant were long stripes of dried mud, five inches high, like thick planks set on edge. These low walls shield shoots and stems from drying winds. We stopped to look. The walls were patted mud; there were fingerprints. There were fingerprints dried into the loess walls around every building in the western city of Xian. There were fingerprints in the cones of dried mud around every tree's roots in large afforestation plots near Hangzhou, and along the Yangtze River. There is good soil in China, too, on which peasants raise three and even four crops a year, and there are 2,000-acre fields, and John Deere tractors—but there is not enough. There are only some arable strips in the river valleys—only one-tenth of China's land. If you look at your right palm, you see a map of China: the rivers flow east, and most of the rest is high and dry; the arable land is like dirt collected in the lines of your palm.

Near the eggplant field, two men were pulling a plow. These humans were pulling the iron plow through the baked ground by ropes lashed across their chests. A third man guided the plow's tongue. "The old planet," Maxine Hong Kingston calls China; it is the oldest enduring civilization on earth.

Now at the meeting, our Chinese colleagues have a question for us. The head man leans forward; the playwright to my left opens a notebook and clicks a ballpoint pen. They all want to know this: which are the best writers in the United States? Whose fiction should we translate for China?

And what, pray tell, can we answer? Which writers, which works? I like Updike: *Pigeon Feathers*, *Rabbit Is Rich*. A Toyota dealer and his wife make love on a bed of gold coins. A major American novel, out of the question. I like Marilynn Robinson, *Housekeeping*. A young girl in Idaho gives in to sloth. What would they make of Pynchon's *V*? The room in which a Chinese reader lives may, or may not, have a single twenty-five-watt bulb. China has little paper, for printing books or anything else. I think of those trees in afforestation plots by the river, by the tracks, those trees one man or woman plants by hand, pats a cone of mud around, digs a ditch beside, waters . . . they're virtual houseplants, these trees; they're pets. How many trees should they fell to print what, and why? Doctorow? Mailer? Roth? Chinese peasants stack hay in the fields, for there are no building materials for barns. Still, we all know why books are worth it. But our books? Today's books?

All our literature does, in the words of the Party journal,

is "express an individualistic and anarchic mentality." "Too selfish for us," one man said earlier.

The work of China is to irrigate land, control floods, make the rivers navigable, distribute grain, lay railroad track, pave highways, electrify the countryside, get more machines.

In the cities, where incomes are five times those in the country, families are saving industrial coupons for years on end to buy a bicycle, or to buy a sewing machine with which to fashion both clothes and bedding from their cotton allotment of six yards per person per year. The family lives in its one or two cement rooms. The wife washes the twigs and stones from the rationed rice and cooks some cabbage on a shared stove. Six days a week the husband and wife put in long hours in their production units; the wife spends two hours a day buying food. On Sundays they bring the baby home from nursery school, where one-third of Beijing's babies live. They all dress up and go to the park, which has several plots of flowers.

"Which works should we translate for China?" We are struck dumb. Our six-person delegation of U.S. scholars, publishers, and writers cannot think of a blessed thing to say. One man suggests *Lolita*. He receives a light, surreptitious kick. We appear never to have heard of any American writers in our lives.

When we entered this building from the street earlier this morning, we saw a remarkable sight. Bent over the building's stone steps were four women of various ages, wearing head scarves. We walked around them. They were crouching, one to a step. They were scratching dust from crevices between the steps' stone blocks. To accomplish this task, they were using toothpicks, and moving only their fingers.

Our interpreter turned, indicated them with a proud wave, and said, "Do you know how those women got their jobs?"

No, we didn't. (Was it something they said?)

"They *knew* somebody!" He was happy to explain. "Each of them knows somebody, or has a relative, who works in this building, and so the friend or relative gets her the job of cleaning the steps!"

The woman pours tea again, and we gain some time. We look around.

Through the windows of the meeting room, we can see the street outside. Some men in the street are working with astonishing concentration at an astonishing task: they are lifting twelve-foot slabs of concrete. Each slab is fifteen inches across, four inches thick. The four men raise each slab without breathing; they carry it by ropes slung between bamboo poles on their bare shoulders. Several of us Americans see these concentrating men lift the concrete; we each let out a private, stricken "oh, god." There must be fork-lifts in China, but we never happened to see one.

What novels have we got that will encourage these people not to throw in the towel? Horatio Alger? *The Grapes of Wrath*?

It is almost impossible, given the sight outside the window, not to say at this meeting, forget it. Go for fork-lifts.

But this is a room full of writers and publishers, and theirs is an old and literate tradition. What might really be pertinent? Erasmus, you think. Aeschylus. John Locke. Calvin. Tom Paine. One American scholar in China this summer told everyone who asked him, "Read Marx."

We ask our Chinese colleagues what they have read. They have all read Herman Wouk, *The Winds of War* and *War and Remembrance*. Many have read Robin Cook's *Coma*, Daphne du Maurier's *Rebecca*, Hemingway's *The Old Man and the Sea*, Mark Twain, Jack London. Some have read John Hersey, Saul Bellow, Ursula K. LeGuin, Walt Whitman, Joyce Carol Oates, Irving Wallace, Benjamin Franklin, Isaac Bashevis Singer, Washington Irving, Howard Fast, Leon Uris. It all comes tumbling out together. (Most of us, by contrast, have read little or no contemporary Chinese literature.) More things develop.

Few, if any of the people in this room are familiar with Conrad, James, Proust, Kafka, Mann, or Joyce. There are of course Chinese experts in these fields, but they don't happen to be here. The Western novel influences contemporary Chinese writers largely through Lu Xun, the great fiction writer of the thirties, who was influenced by the nineteenth-century Russian novelists, who were influenced by the French. In my ignorance I thought that all the world's serious writers paid attention to developments in the novel and in poetry in Europe of the past two centuries. In poetry, because their attention was elsewhere, all but scholars now lack the French Symbolists, Eliot, Yeats, Pound, Williams, Stevens. Okay, but they are translating Longfellow hand over fist, and Langston Hughes. Several poets know e. e. cummings. They all know Whitman. No one has heard of

Moby-Dick, but they have recently brought out *The Year-ling*. The intellectuals have all heard of "theatre of the ab-surd," "stream of consciousness," "black humor;" they seem to reject it all out of hand, as indeed, why shouldn't they?

"Anti-plot! Anti-hero! So many antis!" The man is speaking English. Given the context, he is making good sense. "Our writers write for the great Chinese audience. All this time-travelling, this switching about in time and space —the people are not used to it. Even we in this room—and we are literary workers!—are not used to it. We find it dif-ficult, hard to understand, hard to read. How can you learn what is happening?"

Nevertheless, the Chinese are gamely, surrealistically, translating for publication Virginia Woolf's *The Waves* and Faulkner's *The Sound and the Fury*. They are making up for lost time; foreign literature has long been banned. But I can't help but fancy that readers will conclude that we in the West are a batch of crazies. For how else are peo-ple going to read these novels? For such works readers have no historical context, no modern fiction's beginnings, no theoretical framework but Marx, Lenin, and Mao Zedong. There are no links in the fossil record, no middle layers in the archeological strata. They go straight from Shakespeare to *Catch-22*, as it were, pausing at Washington Irving. It has been only for the past seven years that China has been open to Western literature; now it is filling in the gaps. Very recently, in late 1983, China translated and published works of American literary criticism—the standard studies by Van Wyck Brooks, Alfred Kazin, Edmund Wilson, and Malcolm Cowley—which will surely help clarify some of our literary issues.

I am ashamed to press these points. Few of us in our delegation—and we are literary workers!—know two beans about contemporary Chinese literature. It would even be safe to say, at this early point, that we reject it out of hand. Earlier I tried to read a contemporary novel that everyone I've met has praised for its sheer quality, its boldness and sophistication. I had to put it down. To me it read like fiction from *Jack and Jill*; it had that pre-teen, overexplaining tone. The nonfiction I read seemed much better. Contemporary Chinese fiction, in both subject matter and tone, is an acquired taste (which I have since acquired), and one that requires, as does ours, an historical, cultural, and theoretical framework, outside of which it can scarcely be enjoyed—and within which it certainly can.

Now a certain Mr. Wong casts a new and kindly light on our mutual intellectual misunderstanding and amazement. Mr. Wong has read Maxine Hong Kingston, *The Woman Warrior*. Most of us like it very much. Someone asks him what he thinks of it. He answers in English.

"We think it is only so-so." They hate it. "We think it presents a mishmash. It puts together things from China without making distinctions: superstitions, peasant culture, classical literature, things from very different provinces and dynasties. It presents a distorted view; it is a mishmash." In other words, in his view, it goes from Shakespeare to *Catch-22*, pausing at Washington Irving. Mr. Wong has gentle good manners. He adds, in a softer voice, "But perhaps in America, it is all new, all new and unknown to the readers, and so they like to learn." It's true; we like to learn. And so do the Chinese, who are no more bothered by the chaotic and bizarre impressions of the West that they get from the generous mishmash of books they read than we are by the (alleged) chaotic and bizarre impressions we get from the very few books about China we read.

The meeting is winding down. The jasmine leaves flattened inside our porcelain mugs are drying.

In this May of 1982, things are changing fast in literary circles. Six years ago the Gang of Four fell and the Cultural Revolution ended. Three years ago the state rehabilitated 500,000 intellectuals, including almost everybody in this room. That same year the state sentenced two leaders of the free-speech movement to prison, where they are now. "Scar literature," or "the literature of the wounded," which described some of the sufferings of the Cultural Revolution, has already come and gone; it was too much, too fast. Two years ago the state eliminated a rash of unofficial literary magazines. One year ago, the state banned Bai Hua's film *Bitter Love* and subjected it and him to protracted, if *pro forma*, public criticism. But most writers are more free now to write, speak, and travel than they have ever been in their lives.

Only a few months from now, in fact, the state will honor intellectuals in an unprecedented way: speakers at the Annual Party Congress in September 1982 will add them to the usual list of people who are building China: workers, peasants, soldiers, *and intellectuals.* In the next few months, writers will settle, perhaps only temporarily, an internal debate that is raging in May and June: must a writer depict characters from good classes as uniformly good, and characters from bad classes as uniformly bad? Writers have pledged not to bring up this "intense discussion" with foreigners. By September it is decided that writers may depict "mixed" characters—within, of course, limits.

In the fall of 1983, the winds will shift again; the Party will launch a new rectification campaign to rid Chinese literature of three evils: humanism, existentialism, and modernism. Again there will be accusations, public confessions. Then attention will shift to the problem of the spiritual pollution of writers through contact with foreigners. Round she goes. Where she stops, nobody knows.

To what seems to be the relief of our hosts, we have brought up none of these issues. We have not even answered their question about American writers, except by mentioning some European and Latin American writers, but nobody cares. The room is warm. Several of the Chinese men, perhaps with a fine old guerrilla contempt for propriety, have rolled up their pants, baring their legs from socks to knees. All our hosts are now visibly relaxed.

When the meeting began, they watched us six Americans intently. We do not dress alike—one of us, for a mere example, is wearing a complete cowboy outfit, with vest, boots, and big hat. We interrupt each other; we get excited. We use comic gestures. We disagree with each other in public. A woman may openly disagree with an older man. None of this surprises them; they are sophisticated, and know that foreigners are apt to be churlish. Still, they seemed wary at first, alert, prepared, as if we might start jumping on the furniture, breaking windows, or playing baseball. Their air of expectation was so strong that I, for one, was driven to consider doing just those very things.

But this morning we have provided neither political nor

visual excitement. Instead, our vapid politeness, our blithe egocentrism, our bottomless ignorance, and our misplaced astonishments (Mine: What? You don't know Valéry?) have driven them, during the last hour, to an unrestrained series of yawns.

Now the tension is over and the boredom is over. Our hosts seem suddenly to bestow on us that burst of warmth one feels for departing guests. The lower-ranked men, and the woman, are smiling at us.

The head man probes us one by one, with a deep, knowing gaze. He leans back and concludes.

"We are all completely free to write anything. Our writers are free to write about the darker side of life. But all our writers want to write what the people need. For they love their homeland, and they love socialism."

This son of a gun, this hack, who is lying through his teeth half the time, is going to make me cry, I think. It must be the jet lag. For I am moved by this patriotism, which is real. China is the only one of the world's great early civilizations that still exists—this, in spite of its crippling geography, its beautiful, mostly barren and famishing land. The Chinese people have done what the Babylonians, the Greeks, the Persians, and the Romans were unable to do. By their own efforts, they have kept their country going; they have kept it whole. It breaks your heart to love it, because the people need so much. I am moved by their awareness of the enormousness of the task of modernization, and their awareness that, no matter how many factories they show us, we will notice only the oxcarts and the fingerprints on the buildings and soil.

If this were my homeland, I would love it too, and if necessary lie through my teeth all day, and cry all night, because we are trying to make it all work with bicycles and bamboo. And some of the young people—well, they don't seem to know what sacrifice is.

AT THE DANCE

The Hangzhou Hotel has, to everyone's amazement, a dance band. This is a group of ten young factory workers; they seem to play here every night, knocking off at eleven. The drummer is a woman. There is a clarinet, a saxophone, a trumpet, a trombone, and an accordion.

They play in a long, low-ceilinged, darkened room, for foreigners only. The room has a proper dance floor, many French doors, and three long rows of mostly empty tables. Groups of French, Italian, German, and American tourists wander in, pay the cover charge, drink, and listen, disbelieving, to the music. Maybe—since it's China, after all, and who's to know?—some of them get up and try a tango, or get up and cling to each other while the band tries a waltz.

It is there in the Hangzhou Hotel lounge that we Americans meet a woman: an embassy woman, a woman alone and on edge, and startlingly beautiful. She is tall, and thin, almost forty; her tanned skin stretches over her bony forehead, over her fine cheeks and jaw. Her thin red hair drops straight down her back; she never lifts a finger to it, despite her many other gestures, her pouts, her shrugs, her sudden claspings of her knees. She wears no make-up, no jewelry, nothing in her hair. She is dressed in a loose white cotton pullover top which shows a lot of collarbone, and loose white cotton pants.

"I am wearing my pajamas," she giggles to two of the men. Neither man takes the bait. "Do you dance?" she asks one of them. "I'm afraid not," he says, and leaves. The rest of us drink with her, and dance with each other.

For ten years she has been with the Dutch embassy in Beijing. One gathers that she had a lover there, who hired her from the Netherlands, and who has recently been transferred out—so she has just lost her job, her home in China, and her lover, all at once. Now she is on her way out of China, loose in the world with nothing particular to do and no reason to be anywhere, and bitter about everything. Like many of the foreigners we meet, she has little good to say about Chinese Communism, but she does not want to live anywhere but China. Nowhere else is so endlessly interesting.

We have heard a rumor, possibly exaggerated, and we ask her about it. (Since then, discussion of this matter, long familiar to China-watchers, has become commonplace, even in the Chinese press.)

"Are they killing babies in hospitals?"

"Of course they are! They do abortions in the ninth month, too—handcuff the mother—and if she dies, so much the better. What do they care?"

She draws her knees up to her chin and speaks furiously, with a melodic Dutch inflection, looking away. The innocence of foreign tourists, none of whom will even dance with her when she is so sad, is perhaps wearisome. But she rouses herself. She has, after all, if not a life, at least a temporary audience. My heart has gone out to her.

"In the countryside, all the peasants have IUDs. Every three months their production units have them X-rayed, to see that the IUDs are in place. The X-ray machines are old, very old, and they leak radiation. It takes maybe ten minutes to get a print. If the women get cancer, so what? China has too many fertile women."

She believes what she is saying. I have no way of knowing what is true; it makes sense to listen carefully to what people say and to look carefully at the people who say it.

"A family I know had a daughter. Then the wife gave birth to a son, in the hospital. They were so happy, you know, to have a son. But after a few days the hospital said to the husband, 'Something happened to the baby; it died.' He doesn't believe them.

"Everybody knows this happens. The Chinese call it 'taking the blankets off.' "

The band is going through its numbers: "O Susannah," "Red River Valley," "Beautiful Dreamer," the "Blue Danube Waltz." We have heard these songs in this lounge for several nights running. All day long we hear them on the radio. (A new hit song, wildly popular all over China this June—heard on the radio, sung by children in the streets—is "Jingle Bells," in English.)

The woman talks on, drinking her white wine and rolling her enormous eyes. Her accent is lovely. She tosses her head as she talks and moves her long legs.

"Oh, people are still disappearing in China; don't think that's over. A friend of mine, he was an artist, a painter—a good painter! praised in the press!—but he got a little outspoken. Outspoken, and he disappeared, they sent him to Qinghai, he is painting doors." She seemed to be appealing to us to do something. "Painting doors! And it's all prescribed, how you paint a door: so many strokes this way, so many strokes that way.

"They're all watched every minute—by their production units, by their neighbors, by their families." She began to wail. "He disappeared over a year ago, and that was the finish of him!

"Why do you think they all want out? Who is trying to get out of India? Who is trying to flee West Germany? Who *isn't* trying to get out of China? Party officials use their influence to get their children out, to the United States. They love their children. They want what's best for them. They know they will very likely never see them again.

"Oh, so many men have said to me, 'I would do *anything* to marry you.' To get out, they mean. I always think, I could marry them, one by one, to get them out."

I listen carefully, for I've had the same thought.

"One friend of mine, just eighteen years old . . . I could marry him, go to the border with him, no, go to Amsterdam and leave him there, or stay a week till he got settled, a month, get divorced—he's only eighteen!—and go back for another, and marry the next one. But—"

And here she becomes wild-eyed. She has thought this through a million times; she is furious, waving her arms so her collarbones show, wailing, exhausted, "But I *can't* marry them all! I *can't* marry them all!"

The band breaks into "Edelweiss." Doesn't anyone want to rescue this beautiful woman? "I'll go to Taiwan," she says, looking into her wineglass. "I'll give English lessons, Dutch lessons, if they want Dutch. I'll go somewhere. I only want to come back here, to China." *Bless my homeland forever*, sings the saxophone player, who does not understand English. Three or four couples are waltzing.

SUNNING A JINX

We visit many Chinese people at home. Our hosts are all rehabilitated intellectuals. They suffered enormously during the Cultural Revolution. Now the Party has apologized to them, arranged for them to have good housing, and accorded them freedom from harassment for their remaining years. It cannot hurt them to see foreigners. Quite the contrary: the state has asked them to host us.

It is unnerving to meet these people, men and women whose accomplishments in the arts or in letters made them first celebrated all over China and then made them prominent targets for the purges. Now they are honored survivors. Their suffering—their imprisonment, forced labor, torture, total separation from their families, about whom they knew nothing—was not a passing thing, like an illness from which one recovers. It lasted for years—from 1966 to 1976; it broke some of them, and age broke others.

Now they accept their honored, legendary positions. Some of them have recently joined the Party; some of them enjoy drinking; some of them are still working. They receive visitors often, and face the awkward, one would think, task of displaying, in one's own person, the living object of all the legend, the living vessel of the suffering, the living spectacle of the result of such a life. All this, of course, they handle beautifully, doing what is really the only sensible thing to do under the circumstances, which is to feed their guests many thoughtfully prepared dishes, and praise them for their skill with chopsticks.

We are dining with a couple who met many years ago when both were students at Oxford. They have lived in China since their Oxford days, working in scholarship and the arts; they raised a family. During the Cultural Revolution, Red Guards carried them away to separate prisons. The woman was in solitary confinement for more than three years. The full story of their torments is too personal to repeat; their grief is by no means over.

Now we meet their small grandson, who is wandering in and out, trying to open the long drawer of the big walnut desk. On top of the desk, for now, are bottles of *mao-tai*, Tsingtao beer, and Johnnie Walker. We Americans have been in China long enough, it seems, for we look at their apartment's potted jade plant, its paintings, and especially its bookshelves, as if we had never seen such things before. On the shelves are mostly paperback books mailed from all over the world by friends, and by acquaintances like us, who know that whatever they send will be passed from hand to hand. There are works of literary criticism, many mystery and detective novels, the novels of Graham Greene, and the novels of Anthony Powell. The conversation is animated.

I hear distant thunder. Outside in the stone courtyard, fathers are walking their children before bed. If it rains, I think, it will help; it will help China. It will help water those sycamores and ginkos we see lining every street, and the little pines and cypresses by the railroad tracks. None of these trees stands in anything resembling soil. It is a kind of packed dust. Every day, another of us notices this dust and asks the guide, How can these trees live?

Along the highways—the guide always answers—work brigades water the trees, with buckets. In the cities, the families who live in each housing unit are responsible for the trees on that unit's street. Shopkeepers are responsible for the trees in front of their shops. In short, apparently, everyone is roused to this task, as to many other national tasks; all the trees get watered. Still, I hope it rains.

Inside the apartment, the conversation has taken an awkward turn. There are painful things about our hosts' lives which no one wants to touch upon. It is time to change the subject.

Our host rises and passes a tray of spiced cucumbers. He is delicate, white-haired, careful in his bearing. Now he lowers himself to a low cushion on the floor without moving his arms.

"Tell me," he says, addressing those members of our delegation who might know, "who is winning the rowing matches now, between Oxford and Cambridge?"

So many of our hosts suffered so much during the Cultural Revolution that for some of us their stories start to blur. We meet a singer who walks bent and limping; she and her playwright husband give us a glorious lunch. Is it she who was thrown from a window? "No," someone explains, "She was merely beaten by Red Guards; she had a stroke. It was another singer who was thrown from a window. It is confusing; so many were thrown from windows. Jiang Qing—Mao's wife—didn't like prominent women."

Some of the stories have, from a distance, a certain macabre humor. I talked to a Chinese-American woman living in China. Her brother, who never left China, was an engineer in a factory. One day someone at the factory had a bright idea. We could double production, he proposed, by doubling the speed of the conveyor belt.

It won't work, said her brother, who was, after all, an engineer; the conveyor belt's bearings will burn out. At once the other workers denounced him as a defeatist. They handed him to the authorities, who clapped him in prison.

So the factory turned up the juice on the conveyor belt. The bearings burned out; production ceased. The factory workers notified the authorities, who beat the engineer, charging him with sabotage: "You said the bearings would burn out—we have witnesses—and they did. How did you know, unless you sabotaged them?" If you confessed, of course, you were punished, and if you did not confess, of course, you were punished. The engineer remained in prison for five years. The factory, because of the ruined bearings, was closed for two years.

Scarcely believable is this tale, which I nevertheless have on excellent authority. Red Guards found a Chinese intellectual who had been educated in the West; they charged him with being too fond of ballroom dancing. To punish him they made him dance on a ballroom floor for hours— with a corpse.

William Hinton, that friend of China who wrote *Fanshen*, told Arthur Miller, "I know for a fact that there were instances of people literally crucified against walls, nails driven through their palms, and left to die." People were beaten in blankets, so their welts wouldn't show; children denounced their parents; intellectuals were paraded through the streets with human excrement on their heads, or forced to crawl on crushed glass in front of enormous crowds. According to Chinese figures released since the Cultural Revolution, there were 100 million people persecuted or harassed and up to 850,000 deaths by beating or suicide. Whole villages were exterminated; people's bodies washed down the rivers and piled up in harbors on incoming tides. All this was in full swing in 1972, while Americans were watching Nixon pose with Mao in Beijing. Deng Xiaoping's government now is a model of comparative rationality and humaneness, and everywhere people seem cautiously, cynically, grateful. Sometimes they refer winkingly to the Gang of Four; they hold up five fingers.

Could it happen again? We ask this question all over China; all visitors ask it. Four years ago when Arthur Miller was here, most people said yes, sure, it can happen again and will; we have to clarify our thinking from time to time. Now, to us, everyone says no. "No," an elegant scholar says. His tone is exhausted. "The people wouldn't cooperate again; you couldn't get them to beat their neighbors to death again." "It can't happen again," says an American Chinese Communist. He has staked his life on this hope—a hope based, perhaps, on a casuistry. "The Cultural Revolution was an aberration. It was—" he glares at us—"fascism."

After one such foray into the life of an erudite, gentle, broken survivor, I try to restore myself back in my hotel room by reading a little literature. I'm reading *Recollections of West Hunan*, by Shen Congwen, translated by Gladys Yang. Shen Congwen, who is now eighty, recalls his boyhood in Hunan Province. I expect to read about peasant life under feudalism, hopeless and simple. Instead I read about the country custom of sunning a jinx.

When something bad happened in West Hunan—such as the death of a child—people used to decide, sometimes, that a jinx was responsible. The jinx was always an old woman, and a poor one, according to Shen Congwen. "Some busybody will fan public indignation and this woman will be caught and exposed to the scorching midsummer sun. This is called 'sunning the jinx.' . . . The authorities never interfere. If the woman dies when tortured like this, again no questions are asked." If the woman "confesses" to having cast an evil spell, then, again, she is exposed to the sun for three days. Those who survive are said to be cured; "others die as a result of this exposure, and people believe they have rid the town of a pest. In fact," Shen Congwen confides, "these people are not criminals but lunatics." Which people? He goes on to say the jinxes are lunatics. These old women, maddened by poverty, believe they are jinxes, and confess anything.

Now the peasantry has access to food, medical care, and education. Surely they aren't sunning jinxes any more, in West Hunan or anywhere else. But the machinery is in place for it. All you need is "public indignation" and the sun.

THE SHANGHAI WORKER

One Friday night in Shanghai, my friend Donald Ellegood—director of the University of Washington Press—found himself alone and lost, far from our hotel. He had been to a concert; now it was late, eleven o'clock. He knew he had to get directions and walk back.

Perhaps Donald was wearing his cowboy outfit that

night; I like to think so. At any rate, he is well over six feet tall, has curly hair, and is obviously a foreigner even without his denim vest and Stetson hat. When he pulled out a map to get his bearings, a little crowd collected. One young man who spoke a bit of English offered to walk him back to the hotel—a trip of five or six miles, it turned out. The kind young man was a factory worker. Together they set out through the dark, almost empty streets of Shanghai.

At first the young worker was silent, seeming perhaps a bit nervous. At last, after the first mile, he turned to Donald and asked,

"Do you own a bicycle?"

Donald said no, he didn't.

The worker held himself higher and loosened up. He owned a bicycle, he said; he described it enthusiastically, feature by feature. It was apparently quite a fine bicycle; Chinese bicycles are steel, and built to last.

When he finished describing his bicycle, the worker lapsed into silence again. They walked another mile, another two miles, through the darkened city. The worker seemed to be thinking. At last he brought out in a hesitant voice,

"Do you own an automobile?"

And Donald, the kindest man on earth, and a man devoted to truth, said yes, he owned an automobile.

They walked the remaining two miles in silence.

———

SOME NOTES ON READING

In Beijing Library—the national library—I was standing by the English card catalogue with Song Hua. He is a young and very jolly interpreter, whose gestures are extreme. When he is embarrassed, he covers his face with both hands; when he laughs, he tends to fall over; when he makes a mistake, he strikes himself on the skull with a fist. I liked him.

The Beijing Library has 11 million 100 thousand books, and 200 chairs. We were standing among several dozen of these chairs pushed up to tables. The chairs were all taken, this day as every day; many people were taking notes in minuscule characters on tiny pieces of paper. Most people, in fact, seemed to have located one such tiny piece of paper to bring to the library for this purpose. There is not much paper in China. There are not many books, either, comparatively; Red Guards burned so many. And, alas, most of the people can't read most of the books; the books tend to be in classical Chinese, in old-style characters, and most people read only the modern, simplified characters not firmly established until the 1950s. On the other hand, partly as a result of the introduction of simplified characters, and partly as a result of the Communist party, literacy has soared.

From any public library, Song Hua told me, *people* may not borrow books. People apply to their production units and show good reason why they wish to read a particular book. If the book is not in their production unit's library, the unit gives them written permission to try to get the book at the public library.

"What's a good reason for borrowing a book?"

"You need the information for your work."

"What if you were an engineer and wanted to borrow a book of literature?"

To my astonishment, Song Hua burst into laughter. He doubled over as if kicked, he gasped for breath, he hugged his ribs and stamped his foot. I looked down the back of his neck. Gradually his head rose again; his face was splintered with hilarity. He gave me a sidelong "oh, you card" look, and said, as clearly as he could, "But you couldn't . . . if you were an engineer . . . get to read . . . a book of literature!" And off he rolled again into squalls of laughter.

Naturally I thought I failed to make the question clear. I still wonder about this. I repeated the question in different terms. Same thing. This absurdity was clearly making Song Hua's day. He looked up at the ceiling helplessly, as if imploring a hidden cameraman to help him consider the idea of an engineer borrowing a book of literature. (Did he think I meant literary criticism?) He fell towards the floor again, straightened up by steadying himself on the card catalogue, and answered as he had before.

At Shanghai's Fudan University I talked to an anatomy professor who had toured fifteen American universities. He was impressed by the modern equipment available to students, by the democratic way professors treated both staff and students, and, especially, by the *diligence* of U.S. students. Now, a year after his visit, he still couldn't get over the way students were able to learn directly and independently from books. He said—and his voice was still incredulous—that he had spoken at Johns Hopkins with a Taiwanese student who was taking a physiology course. This student had told him that for that course they were all expected to read: *two books*. The course was only twelve weeks long and met only three times a week. I nodded. The students didn't read the two books in class, but were expected to read the books outside of class, and learn *directly* from them. Students at American universities ordinarily took *four* such courses.

Ways of learning differ, of course. In a country with so many people, so many meetings, and so few books, it makes sense to be able to absorb most of your information through your ears. Stephen Greenblatt, from Berkeley, who taught Shakespeare at Beijing University recently, reported on the solemn intensity with which his students listened to his words, as if memorizing them. New American "styles of learning" studies show that many Americans, like others worldwide, learn better from hearing things than from reading them.

The newest Chinese literature, which depicts the life of educated people, has as an inadvertent running theme a dreary collective description of how different families share desk time. Usually the child uses the desk first, then the mother, and then, after the others go to sleep, the father. All this emphasis on the desk indicates that people are perfectly capable of working alone, as indeed they are. The park benches in China are full of people silently studying books, often textbooks.

I talked with a man in his fifties who had written several novels and books of short stories. "What do you read for pleasure?" He was an educated man of good will, a friendly man; the question bewildered him. "We do not read for pleasure," he said quietly.

My question had gone astray. It was the term "for pleasure." Reading for pleasure is not something a serious writer would admit to doing. A writer reads, of course; he or she calls it "studying," and it is part of work for China. Many writers read widely in contemporary literature, and study classical works like *The Dream of the Red Chamber*, or modern classics like the works of Lu Xun, in depth and repeatedly, in the scholarly tradition which obtains everywhere. In fact, classical scholarship is a safe refuge for Chinese people who love literature for its own sake.

I asked a middle-aged writer whose literary ambitions, love of literature, and breadth of education I thought I knew pretty well, "How many books, roughly, would you say you read a year, on your own?" "One," he said, embarrassed. "Maybe two." He was helping his son study for university entrance exams. He had almost no free time. He and his wife, who had been married for nineteen years, were saving to buy some furniture. Not additional furniture—just furniture.

A Chinese student in the United States reported, gleeful and awed, to his professor at the University of Indiana, "In the U.S., the only limit on access to books is how many times you care to—well—raise your arm to take the book from the shelf."

SAVING FACE

Early one morning in the lobby of the Peking Hotel I meet an American businessman. We sit on the wide carpeted stairs leading to the dining room in the hotel's older wing.

Sam Samson is in the import-export business; he imports all of China's tin and antimony. He had studied China for years, disinterestedly, before he got into business. While we sit on the stairs waiting for the dining room to open for breakfast, he tells me what is on his mind. Here is what happened, he says. He is undoubtedly oversimplifying.

All the chrome in the world, he says, comes from South Africa. South Africa, like Israel, is one of the countries China does not recognize, does not mention. But the Chinese needed chrome; they asked us to get them so many tons of chrome.

We got the chrome. This was about a month ago. They said, "Where does this chrome come from?" "Europe," we told them, so they could save face.

"No," they said. "You'll have to be more specific. Where does this chrome come from?" "Western Europe," we said. All this time, we were in Seattle, and they were in Beijing.

"No," they said. "You must tell us. We must know where this chrome came from."

So I came to China. Yesterday I met with them in person. They had been asking this question for a month. So I came and met with them and said, "Actually, it's from South Africa."

"Oh, NO!" they said. They were outraged. They were broken-hearted. "*Why* did you tell us?"

"Because you kept asking!"

"But you still shouldn't have told us!"

Samson, a young man, has raised his voice. He looks quite as though he might start tearing out his hair. The padded leather doors to the hotel dining room open.

Did they buy the chrome?

Oh, sure, Samson says. They'd already bought it. They needed it.

THE JOURNALIST

Back in the United States, I turn a page of the paper at breakfast and learn that Tiziano Terzani has been kicked out of China. Tiziano Terzani! It has now been two years since that first evening we spent with Tiziano Terzani and his family in Beijing—an evening from which I am still, in some sense, reeling.

The news story is brief. Tiziano Terzani, the Italian-born Beijing correspondent for *Der Spiegel*, has been booted out of China, given the old heave-ho, by Chinese Security Police, on trumped-up smuggling charges. Actually, Terzani says from Hamburg, Chinese authorities were peeved by some articles he'd written for *Der Spiegel* criticizing new architecture in Beijing.

When we met Tiziano Terzani and his wife Angela, they had lived in Beijing for two years. Tiziano was a big man, as handsome and excitable as Angela was beautiful and calm. They were graceful, intelligent, generous people. They had an apartment in the special compound where foreigners are housed. Their son and daughter, then twelve and eleven, attended Chinese schools. With extraordinary kindness, they had privately invited several of us to dinner.

I gathered that the Terzani household was full of people at all times—people of every nationality—to whom Tiziano gave, in animated conversation, his considerable energies: his storytelling skill, his outrage, his humor, his enthusiasm. "I write my best books at the dinner table," he said—with a deprecatory shrug.

One of the few things we knew about the Terzanis was this: when they moved to China in 1980, they were committed Communists. They had lived in Saigon during the height of the Vietnam war; Tiziano had been a U.N. war correspondent stationed there. He had published his war correspondent's diary, and a later book, *Giai Phong!: The Fall and Liberation of Saigon.* Tiziano and Angela were European Communists: thoughtful, well-educated, widely travelled. In Communism they had seen, I imagine, genuine hope for oppressed peoples' seizing their own lives and living in amity, each for the others. They had been Communists, that is, until they moved to China.

We had eaten dinner with them and their bright, lively children. We had met their many and various pet animals —animals which perhaps amused and consoled the family during the intrinsically infuriating years of a journalist's life in China: trying in vain to get information, hearing sad tales, and hurting, by your contact, your Chinese friends, the very people you care for most.

We lingered around the dining-room table drinking coffee. The topic at hand was the only topic: Chinese Communism.

We have been impressed, someone says, by the easygoing ways of the Chinese people we have met, by the smiling multitudes in the city streets, by their cleanness, excellent health, and apparent freedom from both want and fear. Isn't it better than, say, ten years ago?

Tiziano raised his enormous brows. "Better than ten years ago? Sure." He looked around the table grimly. "But not better than thirty years ago."

My American friends, who are Marxists, sat quite still. Our host went on.

"During the Cultural Revolution, people didn't lift up their heads in the streets. Now their production units take them to the Great Wall once a year. That's what they call progress!

"Each one is a little part, a silicon chip, a screw, bolt, in the big machine. They all died in nursery school!

"Forgive me," he added, contrite. He had been shouting, waving his arms around the wine bottles, forgetting to pass things. I was rapt. His children looked bored and amused by turns. He was trying to get it all in quickly. Now he squeezed his big hands together and took another tack.

"Communism is good for winning wars. Communists fighting a revolution are like Christians: they sacrifice themselves! They are for all the good things! You can't stop them!

"But Communism is *not good government*!"

After a fairly stunned pause, someone began, "But China is a special case."

That did it. Tiziano jumped to his feet and began pounding himself on the head.

"That's how it goes! 'Soviet Russia is a special case!' 'Poland is a special case!' 'The people aren't quite ready yet!' That's always their excuse!"

He was pacing the dining room. On the wall hung a series of lithographs: heads of Mozart, Bach, Beethoven. Abruptly Tiziano stopped pacing. He stood stock-still and looked deep past a darkened window. Now he spoke slowly, stressing every syllable, his voice barely controlled:

"The plain fact is that Communism is an abomination that should be wiped off the face of the earth."

He sat down again at the table. He ran his hands over his head. Angela poured him some coffee. She asked us if we had been to the Forbidden City. Their daughter did a cheerful, rather cruel imitation of an old woman sweeping the dusty Beijing street with a twig broom in the wind.

Softly, very softly, we turned to Tiziano and asked, "If you were in India, what would you be saying?"

And softly, very softly, Tiziano Terzani, stirring sugar into his coffee answered, "In India? In India I would be saying they should all be Communists."

That evening we had wondered if he'd better watch his words. We didn't know how things worked, and there were all sorts of people present. "It doesn't matter," Tiziano had said, apparently exhausted: "my views are known." It is illegal for Chinese people to have unauthorized contact with foreigners. "How can So-and-So visit you so often?" I'd asked Angela. This lovely, gentle woman regarded me for a second before she answered: "He has nothing to lose. They have already taken from him his family and his work. Now he doesn't care what they do."

Last year, Angela Terzani and the children left China so the children could attend another school. Tiziano stayed in Beijing and filed articles for *Der Spiegel.* It was these articles, in his view, that got him into trouble.

One series of articles described Beijing's new high-rise apartment complexes; its lead photograph contrasted one such building with Beijing's traditional low tile-roofed dwellings. I haven't read these articles; Tiziano described them as accusing China of destroying its own cultural heritage. To me, the accusation does not seem wholly fair: the housing shortage is acute in Beijing, and the government is poor. But, as I say, I haven't read the articles.

Further, Tiziano had written a report on the touchy issue of Tibet; he heard it had angered authorities. And his children had written for *Der Spiegel* what was probably an unflattering description of their three years in Chinese schools. (The children told us that their teachers encouraged them to report any private conversations among their school mates that might reveal bad attitudes.)

According to Tiziano's subsequent account in *Der Spiegel*

this spring (No. 11, 1984), Foreign Ministry officers warned him, in a gentlemanly way, that these articles hadn't been well received; they were worried about extending his visa. Nevertheless, after a friendly January talk, the Foreign Ministry had extended his visa for another year. Tiziano guesses that the Foreign Ministry's decision miffed Beijing's Public Security Bureau. He speculates that the Public Security Bureau wanted to rebuke the Foreign Ministry. At any rate, it was Public Security Police who seized him on February 1, 1984.

They arrested him without charges; they interrogated him for nineteen hours. Twenty policemen searched his apartment and confiscated, among other things, an address book with the names of some Chinese people. During the apartment search, Tiziano was not, by his own account, in a cooperative frame of mind; there was a bit of a tussle, with pounding and hair-pulling. Police seized his passport and put him under house arrest; for three weeks they interrogated him, threatened him with prison, and "re-educated" him. Finally they kicked him out of China.

In the course of all this, Security Police officers got off some classic B-movie lines, which Tiziano, ever the ironist, has preserved:

"Confess. We know all your crimes. The nation has been watching you for a long time."

"It will go easier on you if you admit your crimes at once. Talk."

"We know everything. We have been informed by your friend X."

"We are the Security Police. We are not afraid of anyone or anything. We have methods to make you cooperate."

The details of Tiziano's re-education, reported in *Der Spiegel*, are interesting. Like any ordinary Chinese person, Tiziano had no recourse but to give himself up to his captors. He was required to write a self-criticism confessing all his bad attitudes. (Chinese students who return from study in the West spend up to six months writing such self-criticisms and confessing the thoughts that crossed their minds while they were abroad.) Tiziano wrote a twenty-page account called "China and I," which detailed, among other things, his previous sympathy for Mao Zedong.

Police sought his cooperation in the re-writing of recent history. Perhaps because they feared international repercussions, they asked him to deny that he was beaten during his apartment search. Tiziano refused. Finally, in a nice, face-saving compromise suggested by a helpful policeman, Tiziano agreed to say that he tried to escape while his apartment was being searched, and since he was "three times stronger" than the Chinese policemen, they had to use force.

After three weeks of interrogation, confession, and re-education, police charged Tiziano Terzani with possession of Chinese treasures he intended to smuggle out of the country. Actually, Tiziano says, he'd purchased the objects in question legally. One was a reproduction of a Tibetan religious painting—a tanka—he'd bought in the Victoria and Albert Museum shop for two pounds. It was a genuine tanka, police said. When he pointed out the inscription on the back—"Printed in London"—they said, "You're a liar." Tiziano owned a five-inch figurine which police claimed was a genuine Ming Dynasty work of art. According to Tiziano, it was only a crude reproduction he'd bought at a Great Wall souvenir stand. And so forth.

At any rate, after compiling charges, police fined him, gave him a cup of tea, shrugged off the ten-year prison sentence they'd been threatening him with, handed him his passport, confiscated his press card, declared him unfit to live in China, and showed him the door.

PART TWO

ZHANG JIE

Zhang Jie, an innovative and controversial young writer, is carrying my Siamese cat around the house. She holds it by the armpits, so it faces the couch. "Beautiful," she keeps saying, enormously pleased. It is an English word she has picked up since I saw her in Los Angeles three weeks ago. "Beautiful!" Her own beautiful face is tight and alight with smiling; her eyebrows are raised.

Zhang Jie and the other members of the Chinese writers delegation are at my house in Middletown, Connecticut. We have all just had dinner, fifteen of us around a Ping-Pong table covered with linen. Now the cat spills from Zhang Jie's arms and runs away. Firmly, Zhang Jie resumes clearing the table, carrying dishes to the kitchen.

She stacks the teacups, humming bits of the Chinese folk songs they have just been singing. "Zhang Jie, for crying out loud, I've got the rest of my life to clear the table, and only one night to be with you here." Someone translates this sentiment into Chinese, and we see Zhang Jie's eyes abruptly fill with tears. She lowers the teacups to the table, walks in her determined, elegant way to the couch, sits, wraps her arms around me, proclaims her eternal devotion, and joins the conversation. When I glance at her a moment later, she has fallen asleep.

Zhang Jie is forty-five; she has a nineteen-year-old daughter. Even now, in sleep, she retains her trim bearing. She sits upright on the couch, her long legs in their slim-cut dark slacks pressed together. Only her round head tilts slightly forward; her eyes are delicately closed, her lips lightly shut in what seems to be an ironic smile. The skin on her face, as always, looks taut and smooth as a child's, and her expression remains perfectly alert, even though she is sleeping.

She wears an open-collared beige shirt and a smartly tailored dark blazer. Often she wears a white silk blouse, high-necked, with a bit of lace on it, and a dashing belted trench coat with a big purple silk scarf tied loosely at her throat. Weeks ago someone whispered to me—and I can certainly believe it—that Zhang Jie is considered one of the best-dressed women in Beijing. It's an unthinkably odd title. In the context of Beijing, it probably means she is a bit of a nonconformist. I often wonder where she keeps her clothes at home; she lives in two rooms.

Her medium-short hair is wavy; she's had a permanent, as have most urban Chinese women under sixty. Always she wears in her hair a thin, toothed-wire band—a purely Chinese object which has no function whatever save a symbolic one: all women's hair in China is, in one way or another, bound.

Zhang Jie is an ardent Communist. She is also the lowest-ranked member of her seven-person writers delegation (although she is not the youngest), so however controversial her writing may be in China, we will hear no trace of controversy here. In fact, since she is so careful in her speech, we may assume that anything she says, in public or in private, expresses a view that is permitted. And of course, more is permitted now than at any time during her adult life.

When she was a senior university student, she was publicly criticized for "showing too much sympathy for the love theme in a Soviet film." Now she writes about love, and champions private emotion, saying rather cryptically, "People are not always objective. . . . Literature has made me a person of flesh and blood and emotion, as well as defects, and without this I would hardly have written a line."

We are on an auditorium stage in Los Angeles, at UCLA, at the U.S.-Chinese writers conference organized by Norman Cousins. It will be three weeks before we meet again in Connecticut. Zhang Jie, who has never before travelled outside of China, is sitting wholly composed and dignified at the enormous, U-shaped conference table. To her left is a Chinese professor of English literature; to her right is Harrison Salisbury, who at seventy-four is easily the handsomest man at the conference, and who treats her with respectful courtesy. At Zhang Jie's right ear is a delicate headphone attached to a cord which leads to a tiny, cunning radio receiver on the table. We all have these. On Channel 1 we get Chinese; on Channel 2, English. In a glass-walled booth above the auditorium's audience are two skilled simultaneous interpreters, who mutter everything directly into our ears.

Zhang Jie is speaking about her goal as a writer: "To instill confidence and courage in the people. I believe this world is not yet an accomplished world." Earlier she said that her writing reflects her ideal: "Life should become what human beings wish it to be."

She knows we Westerners tend to favor a literature written for art's sake, but, a good Marxist, she disagrees: "Pure literature as our purpose cannot exist, because the writer's feelings will have an impact on the material world." In one of her short stories, an old heroic flutist, whose life has been destroyed by the Gang of Four, is on his deathbed. He tells a boy to whom he has been passing on his art, "You must always serve the people with this flute. Music originates from work. It must serve the working people."

Now at the conference table, Allen Ginsberg is talking into his microphone. We have all been asked to give accounts of our writing and our lives. Art, Allen Ginsberg says, must annihilate the distinction between subject and object. One of the ways to destroy the objective base of American leaders is by hypnotic, repeated rhythms chanted. Moving on to his life, Ginsberg talks a little about homosexuality and then describes his 1950s associations with Jack Kerouac and Gary Snyder. Of this life he narrates deadpan, "We began to experiment with various native herbs." Linnaean terms are produced: peyote, *Lopophora williamsii*; psilocybin, *Psilocybe mexicana.*

I steal a glance at Zhang Jie. She is bolt upright; her eyebrows have shot halfway up her forehead. Ginsberg goes on in a soothing, guileless voice which I find very winning. One night he had a little vision. Mr. William Blake stepped into his room, and stood there, and recited a poem. Ginsberg recites the poem. "After that," he continues sweetly, with lovely timing, "after that, I spent eight years in a mental hospital." Big laugh from the delegates, from the crowd. Zhang Jie looks shaken, bewildered, dismayed. She leans forward, her shoulders urgent, as if she would jump up and help.

How she draws our attention, this winsome Zhang Jie! She carries herself with confidence and determination; she collapses into giggles; she dresses elegantly, raises her chin, touches people warmly, cocks her wide head in a rush of sentiment; her eyes flash with sarcasm; she weeps; points an accusing finger, toes the line, springs around on her long legs in their low heels.

Sometimes Zhang Jie is sleepy. We are driving the Chinese delegates rather hard, but they are always game. Zhang Jie has heart trouble, and sometimes takes nitroglycerin. She has just spent several months in the hospital for an operation to her skull—no trace of which is visible.

Zhang Jie's parents were divorced. She grew up a poor intellectual. Her mother taught primary school. She loved books, and wanted to study literature at Beijing University. The government, however, decided that because of her excellent school record she should study economics; China needed bright economists. Zhang Jie has recalled in print, "When the notice for my enrollment in the Economics Department of the People's University came, I secretly wept in my room. However, I went." When she was graduated, the government assigned her to the First Technical Industrial Department in Beijing, where she worked as a statistician. Later she was sent down to the country, along with millions of other urban, educated Chinese; for years she lived in Fujian Province, working in an electrical-components factory.

After her return to Beijing she began writing stories, many of which won national prizes; the government transferred her to Beijing Film Studio. Now she works at home producing filmscripts and writing stories and novels "in her spare time." "The greatest writers," she says at the conference, "reflect the wishes of the largest number of the people."

We are all going up to Malibu for dinner; Zhang Jie and Allen Ginsberg are sitting in the back of the van. Between them, by chance, sits an interpreter. Zhang Jie is dressed to the nines, in a severely tailored blue dress.

How did it get started between them? I witness only the climax: "Mr. Ginsberg!" Zhang Jie is leaning forward fiercely over the interpreter's knees. Her slender shoulders are squared. "You should not think only of yourself! You must live and work so as to fulfill your obligations! Have your goals firmly in your mind. You should not take drugs! Think of your responsibility to society. As for myself, my goals are always clear. My mind is *never* confused!"

Ginsberg smiles his intelligent, vulnerable smile, and tilts his head like the Cheshire cat.

"My mind," he says, with the tiniest shrug, "is *always* confused."

We dine that evening with Jerome Lawrence, who, with Robert E. Lee, wrote *Inherit the Wind, The Night Thoreau Spent in Jail,* and the stage versions of *Auntie Mame* and *Mame.* His Malibu house is a marvel: all the rooms, and all the decks built on many levels on a hillside, overlook the Pacific, as do the pool and courts. Inside, dozens of original Hirshfield drawings and hundreds of lavishly inscribed photographs of actors and singers line the walls, along with prizes, theater posters, and other bright memorabilia from a life lived in Hollywood and the theater world among many friends. What do the Chinese make of all this? Our host, in his shirt sleeves, is informal and affable. He is an American who worked his way up, and whose essentially democratic instincts the Chinese cannot, I think, fathom. Just an hour ago they were astonished that Robert Rees—a UCLA professor, author of several books, and coordinator of the whole conference—was willing to drive the van that brought us here.

What will amuse Zhang Jie? I show her how to find the NINAs in the Hirschfields. I lead her to one of the bathrooms. (Since neither of us speaks a word of the other's language, we are always tugging at each other.)

We stand in the bathroom and admire it. Zhang Jie's dwelling has no bathroom at all; she shares an external bathroom with courtyard neighbors. My house has bathrooms, but they lack, I see now, telephones. There, set very low on the blue tile wall beside the toilet, is a telephone. Zhang Jie laughs. I pick up the receiver, hold it to my ear, and hand it to Zhang Jie, saying, "It's for you." She takes the receiver laughing, and says into it very carefully in English, startling me, "How are you?"

Zhang Jie no sooner arrived at UCLA than she faced, alone, a difficult, paradoxical encounter. She met a group of Chinese students, her compatriots, who were studying in the United States. Emboldened perhaps by a rare chance to confront a member of the Beijing literary establishment, the students put her on the spot. Why aren't writers in China free to write? Why is their work censored or banned if it is critical of China? Zhang Jie, whose own work is regularly

under fire, had to defend the Party line. She left the con-
frontation shaken.

Later, at Harvard, I met Chen Kun, a literary critic working on Modernism. Who in China now is writing the most
interesting fiction? "There is a group of younger writers
whose work has solid literary merit; cautiously, they are
making innovations." Who? "Zhang Jie."

Back at the UCLA conference table, Zhang Jie is making
a fiery feminist speech. She is leaning into her microphone,
speaking softly, as she always does, but forcibly, with a thin
tone, and a completely unself-conscious attention to her
words.

Women, she says, understand people very well. Also,
statistics show that they live a long time, and have great
stamina. As she speaks she pauses at the end of each phrase,
as everyone here does, so the interpreters can catch up. Her
conclusion to this matter-of-fact, impassioned speech, coming between pauses, sounds very like a lyric poem:

> Speaking for myself . . .
> I would say that in my view . . .
> women are rather superior to men . . .
> in every respect.

This brings down the house. Zhang Jie looks up at the burst
of laughter, startled.

Now the battle of the sexes has been joined.

One of the most interesting Chinese delegates is Jiang
Zilong, a young factory worker whose story "Manager Qiao
Assumes Office" was an overnight sensation. Literally mil-
lions of people read it; it was praised; it was criticized; peo-

ple tried to run their factories by its fictive lights. Jiang Zilong feels understandably grouchy about some of this, saying, "This is a tragedy for the writer. What I write is a literary work, not a training manual for the cadres." He is an intense man with a fine, deadpan humor, who is not averse to complaining into his microphone, in good Chinese comic style, that his delegation chief always picks on him because he is the youngest.

Now Jiang Zilong is giving a brief overview of living Chinese writers. He is talking about Shen Rong and her novella *On Approaching Middle Age*—which has been very widely read and praised. He cannot resist an aside: "There has been in China a threat coming from women writers. In recent years they have shown great talent, and incite in male writers great fear. Also they have enormous readership.

"That novel," he continues to grouse, "should have been written by me. She beat me to it."

Later his list of contemporary writers has led him to consider those in Shanghai. After mentioning Wu Chan and some others, he adds, pouting, "There are many women writers in Shanghai—who are quite famous enough already. I am not going to mention them again."

Is Zhang Jie laughing with the rest of us? I don't know; I am watching Jiang Zilong, how wonderfully furious he looks, how willing he is to let his own anger be part of a controlled comic effect.

We are taking a midmorning break outside our auditorium, which is in a theater building. The delegates and members of the audience are milling around in the concrete courtyard, chatting, taking snapshots, drinking tea and coffee, and snacking on watermelon squares and sticky buns.

From nowhere comes a familiar grab at my arm. Zhang Jie drags me across the courtyard. She is tremendously agitated, and exclaiming rapidly about something or other. I stand where she puts me, turn my head as directed, and see, oh dear, an armed security guard.

He is lolling hugely by the door; I must have walked right past him. He is tall and young. In one hand he carries an enormous weapon. It looks like a cross between a rifle and a machine gun. At his hip is a heavy pistol in a holster. In her excitement Zhang Jie has seized an interpreter and planted him beside me.

Calmly I explain to Zhang Jie, through the interpreter, and lying through my teeth, that the guard's weapons are probably not loaded at all; he isn't really armed. (He just *looks* armed.) He is guarding the theater building.

Barely hearing me out, Zhang Jie has rushed off and collared someone else, one of the conference's UCLA hosts. I think, of course, that she is still alarmed. But no; wrong again, wrong all along. She is mustering someone to take her picture with the guard. Her excitement is pure joy.

Zhang Jie leaps to the startled guard and stations herself at his side. She raises her chin, arranges her good legs to their maximum advantage, and adopts the haughty, cool-million pose which is her custom in front of a camera. In fact, she looks terrific. She makes sure the guard's big guns are showing.

He is, I suppose, a rather handsome fellow, this guard— tall, blond, square-built. I hadn't noticed. And it occurs to me only now, as I watch her pose for snapshots, that at the very beginning, when she first grabbed me, Zhang Jie was probably saying, "Will you take a picture of me with the guard?" or even, "Want to see a good-looking guy?"

I chat with the guard a bit after the others have gone inside. He is in his early twenties, big and bashful; he seems embarrassed by his bristling weaponry. "Tell them I'm here to protect them," he says. "I'm their friend." And I am smitten with one of those rushes of feeling for this country which overtake me often when I'm with the Chinese.

Back at the conference table, Zhang Jie is airing one of her favorite notions. It is a notion which, so far as I know, has been permitted to Chinese only recently, to wit, that people, despite differences in culture, have feelings in common. Nothing more astonishes me than to reflect that this truism was, as recently as four months ago, a somewhat risky statement in China.

"Take Mr. Vonnegut," she says. Vonnegut is sitting two chairs away from her. "I think he and I share certain feelings. For example. We are all having our picture taken together. The photographer says, 'Okay.' Vonnegut says, 'No!' And I think, I know *just* what he means. Vonnegut," she goes on dreamily, before we have fully realized that the anecdote is over, "is humorous. He seems malcontent. But I think in his heart he is sad, and needs comfort."

Zhang Jie's prose has a good grip on modern irony. Her most celebrated story begins, in Gladys Young's translation:

I am thirty, the same age as our People's Republic. For a republic, thirty is still young. But a girl of thirty is virtually on the shelf.

Actually, I have a bonafide suitor. . . . I have known Qiaolin for nearly two years, yet still cannot fathom whether he keeps so quiet from aversion to talking or from having nothing to say.

The publication of a short story can be a major event in China. In 1980, this particular story of Zhang Jie's became a *cause célèbre.*

"Love Must Not Be Forgotten" describes an idealized, chaste love which an old woman, the narrator's mother, has borne throughout her life for a man she seldom sees, a man who, from "class" obligation, married another woman. Older critics criticized the story for its Western-style idealization of romantic love, saying, as god knows older people have always said, that if these two had actually married, their grand imaginary passion would have soon gone by the boards, and anyway, what would have become of the wronged wife? And young people in China said, as god knows young people have always said, that such love is true and grand, a possibility very much on their minds, and anyway, China's many loveless marriages are a feudal hangover, and it was high time somebody brought up the subject. The spicy thing about this apparently innocuous story, however, is that it dared to treat—and sympathetically!—love between unmarried partners.

This story, which no critic here or there considers her best work, made Zhang Jie famous. Another of her stories, "Heavy Wings," drew political criticism for its "gloominess." According to Western China-watchers, Zhang Jie, who has been divorced twice, "is the object of much gossip in China's literary scene"—but this isn't surprising, for so is every other writer.

We are eating lunch at a restaurant. I am seated with Zhang Jie and several bilingual people. I chat with the waitress, and try to tell Zhang Jie a bit about the waitress's life, in case she is interested. She isn't. When the waitress leaves, Zhang Jie is frowning. She unfolds her linen napkin, tucks one corner into her high-buttoned collar, gestures, grimacing, towards the waitress, and says, "I think she ought to wear a bib." When the waitress returns, I look at her ruffled blouse. Its top button is high, at her upper breastbone. It is quite a bit higher than mine.

We are having an elaborate farewell dinner at Norman and Ellen Lear's. At one end of the long dining table sits Francine du Plessix Gray. At the conference she has spoken about art and about women writers; she has befriended several of the Chinese delegates. Now she is exchanging a rapid series of contemporary jokes with the Chinese delegation's interpreter, a sophisticated and easygoing young professor of English, named Yuan Henian.

Yuan Henian's grasp of idiomatic English, and of all things Western, seems to us to be complete. He has lived in Toronto and apparently understands our ways—without making them his own. When later I play a B. B. King album for some dancing, he says, "I have that album at home in Beijing." Earlier this evening I asked him what he had thought of the paintings we had seen at the Getty Museum. "Frankly," he said, "they seem less interesting than those at the Louvre. But did you see the seventeenth-century wedding chest, with a painting on it that prefigures Guernica?"

Francine Gray is chatting, at this rather jolly dinner, with this man, this relaxed and knowledgeable Yuan Henian. He has asked her about recent developments in the U.S. women's movement. Francine is making a reasonable point: that American feminism has moved towards considering the needs and humanity of men—that it has largely abandoned its former, formidable rhetoric, what critics called its "ball-busting, cock-breaking" rhetoric.

At this moment Zhang Jie wanders up to that end of the table; she crouches down to await a chance to speak. When she looks bewildered at the English, someone unthinkingly tosses out a quick translation—"You know: ball-busting. Cock-breaking." Zhang Jie jumps to her feet, claps both hands over her ears, and flees back to her seat.

The next morning we ride a bus to Disneyland. The conference is over; most of the American writers have gone home.

The Chinese writers on the bus are all talking at once and laughing. In fact, they are doubled over with laughter. Zhang Jie is breathless and blushing; her tight skin looks as though it will split from sheer hilarity. What is happening? Someone explains. "Oh, everyone is teasing Zhang Jie." He details what happened at dinner the night before; it is news to me. "They're all kidding her, and saying, 'If you don't be good, we'll make you have an intellectual conversation with Francine Gray.'"

DISNEYLAND

It is a sunny September morning in Disneyland. Bands are playing; people are walking with their children and pushing empty strollers; couples are taking pictures. There is a good proportion of people, buildings, and trees.

The Chinese writers, the UCLA conference hosts, Allen Ginsberg, and I have all just seen a movie, *America the Beautiful*, put out by Bell Laboratories in the fifties. On seven big screens the movie showed highlights of U.S. tourism: the Liberty Bell, the Lincoln Memorial, the Rocky Mountains, Savannah, Big Sur. It also showed long, cheerfully filmed segments of U.S. militarism: tanks rolling on parade, soldiers firing salutes, cadets training with weapons at Annapolis and West Point—all to swelling music and rising choruses.

We have emerged, blinking, from this movie and entered the bright Disneyland streets. The Chinese writers seem content to be here. They are familiar with Disney paraphernalia. In China you can buy Donald Duck on pink thermos bottles, Mickey Mouse and Goofy on yellow cotton handkerchiefs. Filmed Disney cartoons are widely known.

A sophisticated and cosmopolitan Chinese writer named Liu Binyan is strolling down the street with Allen Ginsberg. At home in Beijing, Liu Binyan is a muckraking journalist. The target of his muckraking is corruption in high places; it is astonishing that he is free to travel. He is in the United

States on a six months' visit. He speaks English, as well as Russian, Japanese, and Chinese.

Liu Binyan's upright, forceful carriage enhances the grandeur of his leonine head with its curved forehead, wide cheekbones, and strong jaw. He is young; he is at home in the world; his dark suit, remarkably, fits him. For twenty-two years in China he was not permitted to write; he worked at forced labor. Now he is in Disneyland.

Allen Ginsberg, beside Liu Binyan, is walking with his head down. He is sensibly dressed for a hot September day in a short-sleeved white shirt and green chinos. The spectacle of the movie we have just seen has made him gloomy. He says he considers all that military emphasis in the film to be Mickey Mouse.

Liu Binyan, walking so erectly in his fine suit, cocks an ear and says, "Mickey Mouse?"

"You know," Ginsberg says. He is preoccupied. "Mickey Mouse. With the ears?" He wags his fingers desolately over his head. "A little mouse?"

Liu Binyan stands on his dignity. "Yes," he says slowly, in his careful English, "I know Mickey Mouse. Yes. But the film?"

Ginsberg is emphatic. "That was a Mickey Mouse film."

It is all breaking down for Liu Binyan. He has probably seen dozens of Mickey Mouse films. Incredulity raises his voice: "The film we just saw was a Mickey Mouse film?"

Ginsberg, still shaking his head over the film, chooses another tack. "You know," he explains. "Hallucinatory. Delusional."

Liu Binyan slowly lights a cigarette and lets the subject go.

We all come around a corner and a band is playing. We are alone on a broad intersection under blue eucalyptus trees which cast pale and wobbling lines of shadow on the street. Two of us Americans begin to dance.

One of the Chinese men, with debonair smoothness, as if this were what one does every lunch hour on the streets of Beijing, lightly taps one of the women, and they dance. The band is playing Duke Ellington—"Mood Indigo." They dance lightly, formally, grandly, seriously, until the song is over; we all continue on, without comment.

With us today is Y. Y., the daughter of one of the older Chinese delegates. She is a student at Stanford, and has joined us to be with her father, whom she hasn't seen since she left for the States three months ago. She is a big, solemn girl in a broad-brimmed white voile hat. The students at Stanford call her Y. Y. affectionately, because they can't pronounce her name.

At Stanford she is studying physics; precisely, she is studying the Stanford particle accelerator. The Stanford particle accelerator, a linear accelerator, is two miles long—or, as a Chinese peasant measures the distance between villages, six li.

We have just begun a jungle cruise. In a flat-bottomed boat called, unappealingly, *Mekong Queen*, we have cast away from the dock and entered a tunnel of dense and exotic vegetation. The river twists, straightens, broadens; new scenes appear at every hand.

Beside us, a hippopotamus emerges smoothly from the water.

"Look at the hippo!" I say. Young Y. Y., who in the last

few months has acquired a certain sophistication, quickly puts in, "It's artificial."

Things are always jolly when people misunderstand each other. I have made ludicrous mistakes in many places, in a number of the many languages I do not speak. In China people often looked at me aghast when I tried to pronounce a simple hello; I have no idea what I was actually saying. Several of the Chinese writers spoke excellent English. The following misunderstandings gave me enormous pleasure and in no way reflect on the erudition or courtesy of our guests, who were by and large far more polyglot than we, and certainly more polite.

We were luncheon guests at Disneyland's "Club 33." We had a private dining room and access to a lavish and excellent buffet. With us were three pretty Disneyland hostesses, each dressed in a red tailored suit.

The hostess at my table, to my right, was a gracious and shining young woman whose enormous name tag read SUSI. Her sparkling blonde hair was blunt cut and curled in a flip. She had a wide, friendly smile. She had worked as a hostess in Disneyland for seven years.

To my left sat a Chinese official, one Mr. Fu, whose English was very good; we had all often relied on this man's patient good nature and perfect sense of propriety to clarify and ease conversations. Just now he seemed to be engaged in catching his breath a bit, and in distinguishing among the edibles on his plate. The Chinese are apt to take eating rather more seriously than we do, and they are not so given as we to social chatter at table.

SUSI opened the luncheon conversation, having ascertained through me that Mr. Fu's English was excellent.

"Well, Mr. Fu! Are you enjoying your visit to Disneyland?"

Mr. Fu looked up from his plate and smiled. "No," he said.

SUSI froze. Fu went back to his plate, speared a smoked oyster on his fork, and added conversationally, "This is my very first visit."

Ah, a simple misunderstanding. Easily explained to everyone. After that was straightened out, we all resumed eating with some concentration. Following a decent interval, SUSI, with commendable pluck, gave it another go.

"Well, Mr. Fu!" Fu looked up brightly, apparently eager to re-establish himself in his hostess's good graces. "How do you find Disneyland?"

Fu smiled broadly, raised his eyebrows for emphasis, and said clearly and pleasantly, "I find it very messy."

I have seldom enjoyed a luncheon more. It seemed to me that SUSI, in the long run, was having one of her possibly few interesting days. (In the short run, however, this last exchange required some adjustment. "Messy?" SUSI's smile had fallen and so had her fork. "Messy," Fu repeated, alarmed. "A'messy. A'messing." Oh.)

A middle-aged woman named Fan Baoci—"Madame Fan"—accompanies the delegation as its "secretary." She speaks English, rooms with Zhang Jie in every hotel, and, I believe, enjoys herself. She is a tidy, small woman in glasses, and seems to be a very sober and responsible person. I am charmed to hear about her unexpectedly spirited home life:

"My husband loves children, and he loves me! of course; and he has a good sense of humor. He plays the piano, and the guitar, and the accordion; and often at my house in the evening, after work, we start to dance."

Now in Disneyland Madame Fan and I are alone on the street. The restaurant has chilled her a bit, and we are warming her in the sun. People are passing along the narrow street, which is modelled after a New Orleans street in the French Quarter.

A little boy approaches us. He is about five years old, a blond little boy with long bangs. He is wearing blue shorts, a green T-shirt, and a gun belt with two holsters. Madame Fan leans over and addresses him warmly: "What's your name?"

The little boy draws his two six-shooters and, with a grim "I-hate-to-do-this" expression, shoots us, one by one: Pow! Pow! I keel over, so he concentrates on Madame Fan: Pow! "What's your name?" says Madame Fan, leaning down along the line of fire. The boy steps back and draws a bead on her forehead: Pow pow pow! This goes on. I suggest to Madame Fan that she clutch at her breast and die a bit, in the interest of good will, and if she wants the killing to stop; she does, and she does. The boy pops his guns back into their holsters and stalks on down the street, without having said a word.

Thank God, I think, that Madame Fan is not a writer.

We visit "It's a Small World." Our boat passes among tableaux of animated children from "every nation;" they sing and play musical instruments. When we get to the Asian continent, there is no China. There are Japanese children dressed in obis and kimonos; there are Indian children in saris, Filipino children, Sri Lankan children, Burmese children—but no Chinese at all, even though one-fourth of the world's people are Chinese.

In another part of the park we all examine a souvenir stand's enormous rack of decals. Every country in existence has a decal—its name, and national emblem. At last I find China; the decal says "China," but it is Taiwan; it shows the Taiwanese flag. The Chinese, embarrassed for my embarrassment, studiously look away.

Feng Mu, the head of the delegation, a literary critic, is a rather shy, formal bachelor of sixty-four. He has an impressive gift for making beautifully structured complimentary speeches off the cuff. Like the other writers, who are perhaps taking their cue from him, he seems game for any strange thing the United States may throw at him.

Feng Mu is so formal in his bearing that he manages, at all times, to stand with his spine perfectly aligned but canted backwards, away from the world, like a raked mast. Because of this posture, Feng Mu, who is not tall, nevertheless looks down his nose at things, and seems somewhat taken aback. Among his own delegation he is a favorite, not only for his personal qualities, but for the relative liberality of his politico-literary criticism and the honor it has brought him. Among us Americans he is a favorite also, especially for a quality in his formality which I can only call his sweetness.

Feng Mu and some others try the wildest ride at Disneyland: "Space Mountain." It is like a roller coaster, but its cars, instead of dropping, jerk and veer through hairpin turns in the dark. When it is all over, Feng Mu and the others climb from their cars breathless, and compose themselves on terra firma. Feng Mu pats a hand over his hair and restores it to order. He stands absolutely straight and tilted backwards; his legs are formally together; his expression is at once serene and exalted. "I think," he says severely, as if addressing the press, "that unless one has ridden 'Space Mountain,' one cannot truly claim to have been in Disneyland."

Just as in a conference coordinator's nightmare, we lose one of the Chinese. Somewhere in Disneyland, we have lost Chen Baichen. He is seventy-four years old and speaks no English. He has apparently been missing for quite a while before anyone notices; in the meantime, we have taken a train ride across the park.

Chen Baichen is a playwright whose plays came out in the thirties and forties. He is a short, dignified man, broadly built, with large features and a long chin which touches his top collar button. Usually he wears, as do most of the Chinese, a rather long-sleeved trench coat. Apparently their briefings stress American rains.

This morning Chen Baichen and I were alone together briefly at a breakfast table in our hotel. While we waited for our scrambled eggs, he got up to leave for a minute. (He was fetching, it turned out, one of his books for a present.) Politely, he explained in Chinese that he was leaving for just a minute and would be right back. I understood, I said; fine, sure—for all this was evident—but then he remembered that I don't understand Chinese, and took this to mean that I didn't understand him.

So, quickly, leaning over his place mat, he did what Chinese people are constantly doing during verbal misunderstandings: he sketched the characters with a finger. On his place mat he drew the Chinese characters for, I guess, "I'm just going upstairs for a minute and will be right back." In the middle of this exercise he awoke to its absurdity. I had been, in spite of myself, following the Chinese characters' forms raptly—but now he quickly wiped away the imaginary characters with his palm, made a wonderfully disgusted "Bah!" gesture with both hands, and left. I like everything about Chen Baichen, although I cannot claim to know him, and think it rather rum of us to have lost him.

A disagreement ensues in Disneyland: are we to assume that Chen Baichen, wherever he is, is frantic, or at least upset? Some people think that Chen Baichen, having been through two world wars, occupation, liberation, famine, the anti-rightist campaign, and the Cultural Revolution, can probably handle Disneyland. In fact, we learn later, he has calmly made his way to the park's exit and is waiting on a bench.

I have been assigned to comb a section of the park. By the time I meet up with the group, Chen Baichen has been "found" for twenty minutes. Nevertheless I am so happy to see him that I forget all the warnings in the guidebooks and hug him rather enthusiastically. As we part, I see, disheartened, that his enormous eyes are full of tears.

So he *had* been upset to be lost in Disneyland. I was wrong. Of course he had been upset, and was now relieved —who wouldn't be?

Later, however, I learn that Chen Baichen, by his own account, was not in the least ruffled by being lost in Disney-

land. But the warmth of our embraces when he was found—
that had overcome him, and moved him to tears.

The day is almost over. I am in a Disneyland souvenir
shop with my friend Zhang Jie. She has been searching
every souvenir shop in Disneyland for a little Mickey Mouse
statue to take home to her daughter. Her daughter is a nineteen-year-old university student studying Spanish. She has
already bought her a plastic Goofy dish and cup.

Now here is a whole table full of Mickey Mouse statues,
in just the size she has been searching for. She chooses one
and hands it to me. Idiotically, I turn the thing over and read
to her from the bottom, "Made in Taiwan." This will not
do.

"No," she says and takes it from my hand and puts it
back. She picks up another one, a fuzzy one; she turns it up-
side down and reads, "Made in Taiwan." She puts it back,
finds another model, turns it over, reads, "Made in Japan."
"No!" she cries, and drops it on the table.

On this table, in this shop, and in all of Disneyland, there
is only one other Mickey Mouse statue in the size Zhang Jie
wants. She has to have it no matter where it was made;
therefore, she must not learn where it was made. She picks
up this last Mickey Mouse gingerly by the head, carries it
upright to the cashier, buys it, turns away as the cashier bags
it, and drops the bag in her purse. We leave the souvenir
shop, triumphant.

———

WHAT MUST THEY THINK?

"The women in the United States cannot cook," a Chinese novelist had told me at a Chinese banquet. She was emphatic. "Americans are too busy to cook. They eat out of cans." Seated with us was a scholar who had lived in the United States for a year. He corrected her: "Actually, some of the very old women in the countryside still know how to cook."

Chinese rulers throughout history have often seen fit to close China to the West; China is emerging, cautiously, from one such period of closure. So it is not surprising that knowledge of the West, and of the United States in particular, is spotty, even among educated men and women, just as our knowledge of China is spotty.

In 1982, American scholar Ralph N. Clough inquired formally into the attitudes of China's educated elite—and only the educated elite—about the United States. Often people demonstrated their expectations about the United States by showing surprise.

People were surprised to learn, for instance, that prizes at 4-H club fairs are blue ribbons, not cash, and that U.S. young people nevertheless work hard to win them. (In China, prizes are cash.) They were surprised to learn that Americans occasionally devote time and effort to aiding each other, without pay. It surprises many that Americans invite strangers into their homes. It surprises them that American scientists work side by side with lower-ranked scientists, and even with students. A visiting biologist was amazed to have seen only two beggars throughout a long stay in this country. A Chinese law student was astonished to learn that U.S. citizens need no longer own property to vote. Others can scarcely believe that we all know where the President lives.

Over and over again in China you encounter the notion that our democracy amounts to oligarchy, that our pluralism amounts to deep and chronic dissent, that our welter of opinions amounts to chaos, and that the independence of our institutions amounts to weakness and the inability of our government to rule.

(In unanimity alone, many Chinese people tend to think, is strength. At the UCLA conference with Chinese writers, someone asked about Mao. The delegation head fielded this crucial question, saying, "As for Chairman Mao, we have achieved a unanimous view. The Central Committee of our Party has done so." That's all he said. The point was the achievement of unanimity.)

The Chinese elite in the Clough study asked Americans some interesting questions. Why cannot the President make his policies law? (A common reading of the Watergate scandal was: "A group of capitalists who had backed Nixon lost confidence in him and threw him out.") Why can't the government make the press print retractions? Why didn't the Justice Department execute Hinkley at once? If residence permits are not required, how can the government prevent everyone from moving to San Francisco?

And so forth. The Clough report, prepared for the U.S. International Communication Agency, makes interesting reading.

In China there is a rumor about American parents charging their children money. I heard it in Beijing and in Shanghai; I've seen it reported several times in print. When American children grow up, the story goes, their parents turn them out of the house, and if these children return for rare visits, their parents present them with a bill for room and board. The Clough report repeats this story, and adds that some educated Chinese believe also that when parents visit their grown children, the grown children charge them.

It could be that this particular bit of mud has been around for a long time, and that both peoples sling it. Maxine Hong Kingston notes a similar smear making the rounds of the nineteenth-century logging camps: a homesick Chinese worker finally makes his way back to China, only to be charged cash by his relatives for room and board.

Western things are fashionable in China—from songs ("Jingle Bells") to best sellers (*The Winds of War*) to clothing (sign in a provincial shopwindow: "Welcome to buy the 1982 Jane Eyre hat").

Deng Xiaoping's policy, as Orville Schell points out, encourages importing useful things from the West, like tractors; it discourages the influx of other things, like ideas, which might undermine Chinese culture. Unfortunately, ideas have a way of seeping in—or they may inhere in the things, or adhere to them, like seeds in packaging. At any rate, both the idea of profit and the idea of popular broadcast entertainment seeped in thoroughly when China opened its doors. As a result, Chinese people have many opportunities to learn about the West in a variety of ways.

Recently China has encouraged people to listen to Voice

of America broadcasts to improve their English. In 1981 Chinese television ran two American serials, "Garrison's Guerrillas" and "Man from Atlantis." Both were so popular they virtually emptied the streets. American movies are all the rage. People have seen Charlie Chaplin movies, *Shane*, and *Guess Who's Coming to Dinner*. At Fudan University, *vs. Kramer*; they hope that someday they, too, might be permitted to make films about day-to-day problems. Wildly popular all over China was *Convoy*, an American movie which pits truckers against police, or, as it was understood, workers against the capitalist state. (It was a tad embarrassing in China that none of us scholars, publishers, and writers had the foggiest idea what our hosts were talking about when they so enthusiastically invoked *Convoy* and "Man from Atlantis.")

American books are now available. How our publishers' hearts leapt to see long lines outside Beijing's bookstores at dawn! A worker I met on the streets of Nanjing had read Leon Uris's *Trinity*, Margaret Atwood's *Surfacing*, and Howard Fast's *The Immigrants*. Many educated Chinese have read Hemingway's *The Old Man and the Sea* and Hersey's *A Bell for Adano*, as well as Updike's story "A & P," Irwin Shaw's *Rich Man, Poor Man*, Ursula K. LeGuin's science fiction, Arthur Miller's plays. Chinese publishers are not averse to making money, and since they honor no copyright laws, there's plenty of money to be made. They publish, and people buy, *Airport*, *Love Story*, and Sydney Sheldon novels and Robin Cook novels.

Recently the People's Republic of China has published, among many other works, *Paul Mellon: Portrait of an Oil*

Baron, a biography of Rockefeller, and Leavett's *Managerial Psychology*, as well as Poe stories, lots of Twain, lots of Jack London, and Steinbeck, Longfellow, Whitman, Joyce Carol Oates' *Wonderland*, Malamud's *The Assistant*, Welty's *The Optimist's Daughter*. In late 1983, as I have noted, China published criticism by Alfred Kazin, Malcolm Cowley, and Edmund Wilson—and even paid copyright fees.

Balancing this invigorating jumble of books and films, or perhaps confirming the impression they must give of illimitable chaos, are the 100,000 American tourists who now visit China each year. Similarly, American colleges and universities are now hosting 10,000 Chinese students a year, and the nation as a whole receives 100 Chinese delegations a month.

Chinese vistors to the United States, and armchair critics, are not terribly critical of our racism, militarism, or materialism. Nor are they shocked by American poverty. "Chinese visitors in Houston," Clough reports, "when shown slums at their request, refused to believe those were really slums." In Los Angeles I talked to a Chinese student living in the United States. He had driven across the country with friends, poking around, and had seen something that reminded him of home: a Western desert Indian reservation. "Except for the alcoholism, it was just like China," he remembered warmly.

Although returning Chinese visitors generally paint for their friends a rosy view of American life, they are nevertheless duly shocked by our waste, promiscuity, tolerance of homosexuality, drug use, loneliness, and crime. At worst, they're shocked by our inhumanity, about which they have heard much. We're robots. The price of our individualism and independence is human warmth. To making money we have sacrificed both intimacy and altruism. Everyone is out for himself, pursuing novelty, accumulating goods, keeping one jump ahead of criminals, reading pornography. We don't care for our aging parents; our aging parents won't care for their grandchildren; our rich government won't pay for nurseries; we keep getting divorced. We don't know, in short, what life is about. We are rich whiz kids, a nation of computer hackers.

During the UCLA conference, novelist Jiang Zilong reported into his microphone, horrified, a casual conversation with an American father. The father had said, "My son is very busy: when I want to see him, I have to telephone to make an appointment!" "Such freedom," Jiang Zilong said —missing the joking and proud tenor of the translated remark—"such freedom I would rather not have."

In China, I had blundered into a similar cross-cultural snare.

A Chinese textbook publisher showed us middle-school textbooks. Those in the sciences, consisting mostly of diagrams, were easy to follow. There were organic and inorganic molecules and explanations of their atoms' bonding; there was a strand of DNA and, apparently, a full discussion of inheritance in the chromosomal nucleotides. There was a volume of mathematics beyond me. I compared all this with my stepdaughters' Long Island textbooks. They don't know these things. But at thirteen and fifteen they both think well and independently, read complex modern literature of a sort I haven't found anywhere in

China, and write excellent poems, stories, and essays noted for their complexity, irony, and absence of sentimentality.

The textbook publishers asked how their texts compared with American texts. We were seated in a large room full of people of both nations. With the mindlessness born of sincerity I answered that Chinese education seemed to be stronger in the sciences, and U.S. education perhaps stronger in the arts.

Our Chinese hosts froze. Their expressions, and the very joints of their shoulders, turned to ice. The interpreters turned away, deathly embarrassed. There was a stricken, appalled and appalling silence. What had I said?

I had said that the United States—a country full of barbarous whiz kids—was superior in the arts—the arts!—to the oldest and most refined civilization on earth. Since this was patently absurd, our Chinese hosts could only conclude that I was baiting them from sheer hostility.

On her last morning in Boston, Madame Fan was packing her bags. The Chinese were on their way home. I was lounging around her Boston hotel room. For weeks we had had a running, low-level conversation about our countries' ways of life. She was spying on her fellow Chinese delegates, but I liked her anyway. Now I asked, "What seem to you to be the biggest problems in the United States?"

She gave me, very kindly, a bag of dried plums. We talked about those. She packed some books. I repeated my question.

"Well," she said. She closed a suitcase and sat down tidily at the foot of the bed on which I was sprawled. She squeezed her palms together and spoke. "The old people in the United States—they like to live alone?" There's a polite lady. We talked about that for a while. Then, carefully watching my face, she brought up something else.

"We have heard," she began tremulously, "we have heard that there are . . . a few young people . . . only a few! . . . in the United States who . . . don't really care about their country? But only about themselves? Of course," she rushed on, "we don't know if this is true. It is only something we heard."

At home in Connecticut I met a Chinese economist who had studied in the United States for two years. He listed three negative things about this country, saying that if he could ever get his kids out of China to live here, he'd be sure to warn them about them: "Crime, drugs, and the people's loss of faith in their system."

On request, he explained the last. He had been following U.S. public opinion closely, studying *Newsweek* and network polls. Americans have "found out," he said, that production in our auto industry is not so good as Japan's. The people are very upset about the economy, and list unemployment and inflation as their main concerns. "They know," he inferred, "that the system does not work."

Similarly, in China one of us remarked to an interpreter that many Americans feel that our private businesses are exploitative. The interpreter responded impatiently, out of apparent boredom, "Yes, I have many American friends and I have understood for a long time that the people have no faith in their system."

At a restaurant banquet in China, a playwright allowed himself to express outright anger at the folly of capitalism. It was a strange conversation.

Li Fang, a prominent playwright, was a tall, thin, middle-aged man with long ears. We had spent several days with him in Nanjing and knew him as relaxed and prone to good-natured joking. He had ridden out the Cultural Revolution in relative peace, serving only six years' enforced labor in the countryside, where he sowed, irrigated, and harvested wheat by hand. He was now enjoying rehabilitation, and had recently returned from a four weeks' tour of the United States. In this country he had visited the Midwest and seen something of U.S. agriculture.

"Chinese peasants have many skills," he said for openers. "American farmers have no skills."

This was not ordinary banquet chat. Three waiters appeared, bearing Peking duck, scallions, hoisin sauce, and steamed wheat buns. Li Fang prepared for me a special serving, and went on.

"In the United States I saw excellent land," he said, "land good for both agriculture and animal husbandry. And the farmers there were growing only grasses for hay—no corn!

"I said to the deputy governor of the state, 'Why don't you grow corn? Everybody knows that corn is the best feed for cattle.' He said, 'Because corn prices are down. Corn brings less on the market than it costs to grow.' "

Li Fang made an angry, dismissive gesture with both hands over the restaurant table. "And there you have it. The whole country is crazy. It is a perfect example of the country's craziness. The farmers don't grow corn because of money—when they *could* grow corn, and the cattle need it."

It all seemed a great pity. Of all possible examples of American profit-oriented mismanagement, Li Fang had picked the feeding of cattle. Ashamed, I wondered how many pounds of corn-fed beef I'd eaten in my life, or Americans eat a year.

Our astonishing wealth of arable land is nothing we earned. The pathos of China is its paucity of arable land: per person, there is about a quarter acre—the size of an American home lot. It is this pathos, perhaps, which prompted Li Fang's anger: what couldn't they do with such soil!

Months later, driving through the wooded hills of Connecticut, Li Zhun, the best-informed of the Chinese writers, asked, "Who takes care of all these trees?" Li Fang himself, I heard, had asked a Midwest farmer, "How do you irrigate all these fields?"

Now at the banquet, Li Fang was continuing, mightily irritated. He had pushed back his chair and stopped eating.

"The deputy governor couldn't even tell me the ratio of husbandry to agriculture in his own state!"

Lamely, I tried to defend this unknown deputy governor, saying perhaps he didn't specialize in farming. "That's right. He knows nothing about farming. And the people don't like him. I talked to several citizens, and they were all against his policies."

"Don't take that too seriously—we always criticize our leaders. It is our hobby, our sport."

Li Feng all but growled. "We also criticize our leaders," he said.

While the Chinese writers were visiting the United States, I read the newspapers with a fresh eye. Every day the Los Angeles hotel delivered a newspaper to each room. This happened in China, too, but there we got the "Good News Gazette," *China Daily*, in English. Just a month before our visit, the government had reprimanded *China Daily* because it had reported a flood in China.

Here is what we, and presumably our Chinese guests, read in Los Angeles:

—A man allegedly spanked his two-year old son to death with a paddle, in front of twenty unprotesting witnesses.

—"About 30 percent of American homes were hit by crime last year."

—Los Angeles indicted ten people for "masterminding an Indonesian 'slave ring' that placed domestic workers in the homes of wealthy Beverly Hills residents."

—Headline: "Transsexual Murder: A Tangled Trio."

—Headline: "How Can America Again Compete in World Markets?"

—"A Southwest Los Angeles man who raped a 12-year old schoolgirl, asked her forgiveness, prayed with her and then raped her again, was sentenced . . ."

The usual. We never discussed these newspapers. So I never got to try to explain why, despite these evils, so many of us have not "lost faith in the system."

NOT TOO EASY

Home in the United States I had time to look into the colorful batch of English textbooks which a Chinese publisher had given me. These little soft-cover books, printed on paper which turned brittle and brown in twelve months, teach the English language to Chinese middle-school children. Their assumptions are worth examining.

Like most children's books they stress kindness, cooperation, diligence, resourcefulness, ambition, cleanliness, and sharing. The textbooks freely ascribe these qualities to English-speaking foreigners ("Tom, Mary, Mr. Baker") as well as to Chinese people.

About the United States some texts seem to strive to be fair. Although the advanced story called "A History of Negroes in America" implies strongly that, at the time of the Civil War, Northerners favored abolition of slavery because they wanted blacks for factory workers, and although it implies strongly that southern Americans are all and uniquely prejudiced (a misapprehension which many Americans share), the story nevertheless concludes generously, even misleadingly, "In the 1960's things got better. New laws were passed. . . . Today, at least in the eye of the law, blacks and whites in America are equal."

In another story, a black American girl "speaks her mind." Her father has lost his job; the family is on welfare. "Something must be wrong with this country." Her parents, who are, remarkably, illiterate, get bullied and cheated everywhere. She works hard at her lessons so that ultimately no one will dare cheat her. "I'll fight," she says. In the pictures, she and her mother, who resembles Aunt Jemima, wear head scarves. In this story and in another story, U.S. blacks are shown picking cotton.

There is a vivid description of a garbage strike—the smells, the rats—and a nice English-speaking family wondering why the government is powerless to end the strike and why the public won't recognize that garbage workers perform an important service.

Most pointedly, there is a vivid parable which attacks the claims of democracies to free speech. This is for advanced students of English.

An American, wonderfully named Mr. Hornsnagle, visits a country called Yap Yap. The ruler of Yap Yap is proud of its policy of free speech. He takes Hornsnagle to a meeting. When an issue is called to a vote, four rich men raise golden trumpets and make a loud noise in favor of the proposal. The many poor people, who are against the proposal, have no golden trumpets, so they can't make any noise; the proposal carries.

Hornsnagle is not impressed. He says, " 'In America, instead of golden trumpets, we have newspapers, magazines, and radio stations.'

" 'That's very interesting,' said the ruler. 'But who owns all these newspapers, magazines, and radio stations?''

" 'The rich,' said Hornsnagle.

" 'Then it's the same as Yap Yap,' said the ruler." A long series of questions makes sure the students get the point.

Throughout the texts, the foreigners' system is bad, but the people are good. The texts for younger students, especially, show English-speaking people acting decently towards each other. Family members care for each other and children share with their friends. Even people in authority are just and kind—and this comes out in a remarkable way: Both factory bosses and teachers apologize to their charges when they have falsely accused them.

False accusations are a bit of a running theme in these textbook scenes—perhaps a legacy from the years of the Cultural Revolution. People whose English is good enough to write textbooks likely have had some experience of false accusation during those years, experience fresh in their minds.

Jenny is late to school because she stopped to pick up and return somebody's lost wallet. Her teacher chews her out in front of the class. She doesn't try to defend herself. When her teacher learns what Jenny has done, he apologizes to her in front of the class.

In this story, people of good will easily patch up the public damage caused by false accusation. In another story, however, the patching-up effort fails. This is an oddly complex, violent, and unresolved narrative.

His fellow workers falsely accuse young Johnny Ford, a mechanic, of stealing. When at last the boss learns the truth, he says, " 'Johnny, I want to apologize—for us all. Please stay with us. The lads now know that you aren't a thief.'

" 'Thank you, Mr. Smith. But I can't work here any longer,' replied Johnny Ford."

And that's the end.

In the course of this remarkable and gritty story, it is revealed that Johnny has actually just been released from prison—where he was sent for theft. Further, Johnny gets so angry at his chief accuser, Bob, that "when Bob tried to catch hold of his arm, Johnny hit him in the face. Bob fell to the ground with a bleeding nose."

Exercises: "Why did Mr. Smith give Johnny a job although he knew that Johnny had been in prison?" (Answer, from the text: "He was honest. Since a lot of people make mistakes in life, Mr. Smith wanted to give Johnny a chance.")

"Why did Johnny hit Bob?"

"Is it right to say, 'once a thief, always a thief'?"

"What have you learned from the text?"

Notes: . . . Johnny hit him in the face. . . . 约翰尼打他的脸。

Bob fell to the ground with a bleeding nose. 鲍勃倒在地上，鼻子流着血。

介词短语 with a bleeding nose 在句中作状语。

Westerners in these textbooks are mostly people with pleasant expressions and curly hair. Western people, even children, and Chinese people have no interchange whatever. Carl and Mike talk, Sally and Mary talk, Wu Dong and Li Hui talk, Li Pin and Wei Fang talk, but, in four textbooks, Carl and Wu Dong exchange not a word.

(In China a young woman of eighteen told me how she and her friends were taught, as tiny children, to regard foreigners. Her parents were intellectuals and Party members. "They said we should be nice to them." Could you, or can you, ever regard foreigners just as people? "Never," she whispered.)

In one rather grim story for younger children, some boys and girls are playing at soldiers. They have wooden guns.

Under a tree is their target. "It has a very ugly face."

The big boy is saying to the little soldiers, "Look at that man. He's our enemy. Fire your guns at him!" In the picture, the target's face has bulging round eyeballs and a long hooked nose. It looks like Henry Kissinger.

There are several songs:

> Beloved Party we thank you
> For our happy days. . . .
>
> O Chairman Hua
> Our wise leader,
> We'll work hard together. . . .

In these texts there are no stories which take place in China's past. (There are some Western period pieces, however—a nicely-done *Gulliver's Travels* in Lilliput, and a sketch of Thomas Edison's boyhood, in which Edison invents things, saves lives, scorns school, and sells candy, sandwiches, and newspapers.)

China's present, in the texts, is calm and forward-looking. Young people work hard and share. They eagerly buy tickets for an evening lecture called "How to Protect your Eyesight." They admire peasants, soldiers, workers, and intellectuals. A little girl's parents forbid her to read in bed, for reasons unclear. People watch television programs broadcast by satellite: "This has helped the people of China and other countries to understand each other better." China is in the process of becoming. "The communes are using more and more machines, and they are getting in bigger and better crops."

A bright future is a crucial theme. It is a future, I infer,

in which China shares in the world's technological marvels
—marvels mostly depicted, for children, as toylike gadgets
suited to urban life.

Charlie is sick, so his mother sits him in front of a
"visionphone" and calls the doctor. The doctor diagnoses a
cold and (appealingly) gives him an excuse from school. In
another story, the same Charlie is well. He sits at the visionphone, calls the library, and requests a book about basket-
ball, the pages of which appear on his screen. When he
finishes reading a page, he commands, "Turn!"

Sally and Mary talk about Sally's ambition to go to the
moon as an astronaut. Nothing Mary says can erode Sally's
ambition.

Due to a quirk in the design of the textbook series, the
brilliant technological future appears to be entirely in the
hands of Westerners—but the textbook writers do not, I
think, mean to make a point of this. Rather, the texts for advanced students cast *all* their stories with Western characters.

Finally, in a late story in the most advanced text, there is
a moving piece narrated by an imagined student of English,
presumably a student who has followed the course of study
in these matching textbooks for years. The student says,
rather forlornly, and to no one in particular, "We can understand some English. . . . We can read a little English, too.
Look at this passage.

. . . We are working hard to make our country rich and
strong. In about twenty years, China will become a modern
and strong socialist country.

"This passage isn't too easy," the student comments. "We are happy we can understand it now."

SINGING THE BLUES

"American songs have no feeling, no depth," the intense young writer Jiang Zilong says. "They are too bouncy—not subtle."

Several times during the Chinese writers' visit to the United States, this young man has, upon request, started singing after dinner. His protests—that he will not sing, he cannot sing, he never learned to sing, we should not pick on him—are faint; he is already gearing himself up for the performance.

Jiang Zilong is tall, broad-shouldered, handsome, with a slightly thrusting jaw, long arms, an intelligent expression, and almost violent gestures. Now, in my crowded Connecticut dining room, he scrapes back his chair and stands. He tosses his head, jerking back the damp hair on his forehead; he removes his jacket, walks behind his chair, fastens his fists tightly to the chair's back, leans deeply forward from the waist, and stretches; then abruptly he straightens, locks his hands behind his back, tosses his head again, and, with a fierce expression, sings.

The long melody winds down and down, with controlled quavers; it lightens and rises, then slowly warbles off to the side in a baroque and unmatched series of curls. Jiang Zilong frowns at the ceiling. His jaw has opened only slightly. His voice is strong, his concentration perfect.

The long melody is winding around the dining-room walls like a painting on a scroll unrolling, a painting whose vision enlarges without ever repeating. There is a village of unfamiliar complexity, deep in a river valley curving between dark mountains, where only the light of sun, moon, and stars reaches directly, and where a young woman kneels at her doorstep, missing so much an absent man, an older man. It is the hundred empty chambers of her heart with their unexpected turnings that the melody's bent and tremulous shafts are exploring. Down at the other end of the long table, I notice suddenly, a very much older Chinese writer is stamping time on the floor with his foot.

The song ends, seemingly cut off in the middle—perhaps the man she longs for has come to her, after all?—and Jiang Zilong stands fine-tuned but at ease, rolling up his shirt sleeves before he sits again, unsmiling, all alive.

Yuan Henian sings. He is the young, relaxed professor whose knowledge of the West is so astonishing—who owns the B. B. King record, who knows a stack of Polish jokes. His is probably the best voice in the room, a rich, vibrant baritone. He sings with his hands in his pants' pockets, Sinatra-style, one leg thrust loosely forward, head thrown back, smile never absent; he exults.

Zhang Jie sings. Modestly, she does not rise. She sings as she speaks in public, matter-of-factly and unself-consciously, seeming to be more interested in doing a careful job than in playing to a crowd. Her voice is high, thin, and pure. Her face lifts and stays lifted, smiling and alert. She, too, barely opens her mouth, but instead sings and smiles through lightly closed teeth, almost like a ventriloquist.

One of us Americans sings a bouncy little novelty song, suitable for children. Yuan Henian translates it, just as he has translated the Chinese songs.

Three weeks earlier in California, we and the Chinese writers sang together the standard Chinese repertoire of Western songs.

Returning in a bus from our trip to Disneyland, we all sang, perhaps humoring each other, "Home on the Range," "Edelweiss," "Red River Valley," "Auld Lang Syne," "America, the Beautiful." The Chinese learned these particular songs when Nixon visited; loudspeakers played them, events were televised, and the songs caught on. That day on the bus we searched around for something else we could all sing. We found "Village of Sorrento" and "Santa Lucia."

Zhang Jie was sitting just behind me in the bus. She leaned forward and suggested "O Sole Mio;" she began to sing it, quite evenly, in her high, thin voice, appealing to me to join her in the Italian, and disappointed that I could not. Zhang Jie, according to her biography, grew up with Western music. She sang on, her shining face full of all the range of emotion that her voice lacked; and now, weeks later, that moment is beginning to haunt me, that moment on a bus coming back from Disneyland, when Zhang Jie sang "O Solo Mio" between her small closed teeth, beaming; when I was so full of feeling myself, so incompletely expressed, and Zhang Jie was singing, by rote, in such tight, almost staccato notes, "O Solo Mio."

On that bus, as everywhere, Allen Ginsberg carried a tiny, hand-pumped box-organ, in a red leather case the size of a shoebox; he got it in India. He put it on his knees and pumped its leather bellows with his left hand; with his right hand he pressed the octave and a half of piano keys. To my increasing admiration, Allen Ginsberg did not know, or professed not to know, the very popular American protest songs of the thirties and sixties. He was, however, willing to spin off a witty and poignant improvisation, a present-moment blues, about being in a traffic jam on the L.A. Freeway coming back from Disneyland.

We were jamming these blues contrapuntally with our voices and the little box-organ. When the Chinese writers grasped that we were winging it—singing almost faster than Ginsberg was pulling the lyrics out of thin air, out of the very highway billboards as they appeared—then, slapping their knees, they all began to sing, any old words or la la la to those blues progressions known in the bones of almost every adult on earth. They were laughing, I say, and by god they were belting it, all those solemn old Chinese Communist Party members; they were belting, and rocking their shoulders, and opening wide their jaws.

Now, later in the evening in which people sang solos after dinner, we are walking across the campus of Wesleyan University. The Chinese writers will sleep here, at a guest house. With me is one other American, Jay Henderson, from the National Committee on United States-China Relations; he is shepherding the Chinese delegates around the

East Coast, and has brought them here. Tomorrow we will all go on to Concord, Boston, and Cambridge.

Jiang Zilong, the intense young novelist, makes his remark: "American songs have no feeling, no depth. They are too bouncy—not subtle."

It is late, and dark. By street lamps we see pumpkins on the neighborhood porches and stoops. We pass under old copper beeches, silver-skinned even in this dark, which cast their doubly dense night over us as we walk the Chinese writers to their rooms. It is warm. The air beneath the trees smells sweet and ripe, like a bag of corn.

What have we got? For Jiang Zilong we two Americans sing "Star Dust." Passing through the moist and unseasonable night, under the widely spaced and trembling copper beeches, we sing "House of the Rising Sun;" we sing "St. James Infirmary."

"That's better," says Jiang Zilong.

ABOUT THE AUTHOR

Annie Dillard is the author of a book of poems, *Tickets for a Prayer Wheel*, a book of literary theory, *Living by Fiction*, a prose narrative, *Holy the Firm*, and a collection of essays, *Teaching a Stone to Talk*. Her first book of prose, *Pilgrim at Tinker Creek*, won the 1974 Pulitzer Prize for general nonfiction. She lives in Middletown, Connecticut with her husband Gary Clevidence and her daughter Rosie.

———